T0114761

THE PAINTED FLAWLESS MANUAL

The Art of Intimacy

EKANEM KOFI IKPEME

WESTBOW
PRESS®
A DIVISION OF THOMAS NELSON
& ZONDERVAN

WestBow Press books may be ordered through booksellers or by contacting:

WestBow Press
A Division of Thomas Nelson & Zondervan
1663 Liberty Drive
Bloomington, IN 47403
www.westbowpress.com
844-714-3454

Scripture quotations marked AMP are taken from the Amplified® Bible, Copyright © 1954, 1958, 1962, 1964, 1965, 1987 by The Lockman Foundation. Used by permission.

ISBN: 978-1-6642-9440-0 (sc)
ISBN: 978-1-6642-9439-4 (e)

Print information available on the last page.

WestBow Press rev. date: 03/28/2023

Contents

Preface

Sometimes my delight from an experience has been tainted by the image I held of myself. So what on earth gives me the right to write a book about self-image, identity, or intimacy with self? I think the fact that I admit I am not perfect, but am on a journey to realizing that perfection, is what qualifies me.

In 2021, just after my fortieth birthday, I started a blog that eventually led to me starting a podcast as we were emerging from the COVID-19 pandemic. Many things had changed in my routine during that season of my life. I never anticipated I would start a podcast. I had always loved writing, but podcasting was a completely different ball game—new territory—one that obviously had been well-tapped by others, but not one I had ever considered for myself. What started as me simply speaking to others eventually led to me inviting family and friends to speak on my podcast. By the third quarter of 2022, I had the framework of *The Painted Flawless Manual* on my computer staring back at me. By December 2022, I had signed a publishing contract.

I tell you this for a few reasons:

- I am not quite sure how this all happened. I know I have always wanted to write a book, but I didn't think I would write non-fiction or that it would happen as it did. Yet so much learning has come from this, and in addition to that, much of my forty years of living have been poured into this book.
- I am on a voyage of self-discovery. This whole process of writing and podcasting has been a journey of discovery. I didn't write this book to say I have arrived in my knowledge and understanding, but I am on a journey to my own destination. I think that is the way we should look at life, so that we don't make it a whole lot more complicated than it ought to be.
- I think it is important to share some of this truth I am learning and grow with others too.
- I wanted this book to flow almost like an earnest release to an old friend in a brave space. I hope I have achieved that.

This book includes snippets from my own progress on self-discovery: understanding my self-image and the importance of staying true to it and the power it carries. It was birthed from a wrestle within me, and I found many people have those moments of wrestle too. In fact, what was revealed in that season of my life was that many were dealing with a hidden pandemic—the pandemic of the twisted self-image. Many of us have struggled or are struggling with our self-image, our value, our direction, and how to be the one and only version of ourselves that is true. The issues of racism, depression, broken relationships, and many other global issues stemmed from one source—who we think or believe ourselves to be.

The word "intimacy" is derived from the Latin word *intimus*, which means "inner" or "innermost." This intimacy begins with self. When we have deep intimacy with self we understand and appreciate our innermost qualities. We are able to bond on many levels in the appropriate way and cultivate healthy relationships.

I am discovering on my sojourn that "my presence" is the biggest asset I own. It is the basis for everything my life is hinged on. It is immensely powerful, yet we sometimes take it for granted, and some of us are not even aware of it. The people we talk to, the friendships we cultivate, the odd connection we make each day whether at home, at work, in church, or on the street—these encounters all happen in your presence (you are not absent from them). Your presence carries its own unique frequency and potential to attract or repel.

It is important for each of us to take time to explore and realise our own self-image. In doing so, we also get to appreciate the journey of others that remain separate and unique. Understanding our separateness yet solidarity remains a fundamental building block to dismantling some of the systemic issues we may face today.

Our minds are a powerful force in this voyage of discovery—we must guard them fiercely. They are the filter through which our everyday decisions are made.

In the eyes of our Creator, our self-image goes much deeper than the surface of things, and what we know of it is constantly evolving, deepening, as our knowledge of God keeps increasing and growing on this adventure with Him. How we arrive at the truth of this requires an exploration of intimacy with ourselves and with Him.

So really, as long as we stay with Him, abide with Him, and grow with Him, our self-image should grow stronger and clearer with every passing day, but never to the point where we think we finally know it all. It could never be that way as long as we walk on this side of eternity.

The book of Proverbs says a stable self-image requires righteous counsel.

It is that counsel I sought as I began the journey of *The Painted Flawless Manual,* and it is that same counsel I continue to seek out as I continue my personal, spiritual journey of peace, value, and empowerment.

Be blessed.

Introduction

I hope this book provides a basis for understanding the value in our self-image. It helps identify the many layers that form significant parts of our being. It reveals wisdom nuggets from lived experiences and those of Biblical heroes. These lessons can help us push through wrestling moments and claim our true identity.

Ultimately, the first part of *The Painted Flawless Manual* enables us to discover or rediscover ourselves through our unique rhythms and deep reflection, even when we might have thought ourselves completely unworthy.

This book is divided into five areas.

First, the idea of intimacy and value—See into Me. This chapter gives us the opportunity to explore the concept or possibility of seeing or knowing all of who we are, not just on a personal or superficial level, but much deeper—call it spiritual if you like.

The chapter that follows presents The Wrestle, which we sometimes encounter as we dig deeper into ourselves as we begin to interact with our environment, people, and structures around us.

This necessitates Owning My Identity, which entails being aware of who you are and owning your strengths and weakness, quirks, and how you can be effective in your own identity.

When you understand what you are dealing with, you need to then find your own unique Rhythm and Pace to meet your purpose and continue in the journey of becoming whoever you aspire to be.

The final chapter, The Power of Deep Reflection, is how we can play over what has transpired and consider areas we can improve upon, understanding that true reflection is not necessarily what others have to say about us but what we have to say about ourselves when we do this in close relationship with God.

This has been such a benefit in my journey. Approaching rediscovering myself in this way has brought growth, appetite for the right things, empowerment so that I have capacity and capability to be a source of help to others, the ability to operate in peace even when the environment is chaotic, and finally, a renewed sense of worth. This is something I continually must do, which is why I wrote this as a manual. I can review it and practice the steps again and again when I need to renew my thinking about who I am or my direction, or if I just need to reset my priorities so I keep in tune with my rightful image.

At the end of each chapter, you will get the opportunity to quiz yourself. This can be done in private or as part of a group, which could be more fun and rewarding. I hope you will do this in a brave space that encourages you. It can be used to facilitate group activities, and it is laced with Bible verses for reference to truth found in the story of many Biblical heroes and heroines.

Each chapter also has what I call "Flawless Finish Pointers," which help to summarize the chapter and highlight thought-provoking concepts the reader can meditate on as they reflect inwardly.

This book greatly helped increase my self-awareness and self-management. I am finding my own rhythm and pace, which I believe are unique to everyone but can be harmonized with others; they also change depending on your season of life. They help position me to succeed in life and bear well when I don't. They have helped position me for more productive relationships/connections and cultivated a conducive environment that continues to stimulate my growth and provide room for new opportunities in my life. I hope you will find this book does the same for you and much more.

Chapter One

SEE INTO ME

━━━━━━━━━

I once had the privilege of seeing the *Mona Lisa* painting at the Louvre Museum in Paris. It was quite the experience. As I attentively circled the front of the knee-high metal barricades that sectioned people off from getting too close to the painting, I marvelled at the portrait of this woman who was literally no one of real consequence. Above the shuffle and whispers of people as eager as me to see this famous piece of art, my memory replayed the many rumours I had heard about the painting over the years. I'd heard tales about the stare of her eyes that filled with sadness, along with the hint of a smile that could light up your darkest thoughts. I'd also heard numerous tales of what she was really like beyond what was portrayed, and even rumours of a love affair with her painter.

The woman captured in the *Mona Lisa* had been cast by

many as the quintessential beauty. But as I stared at her in that museum those many years ago, she seemed surprisingly ordinary. Her attire, the plainness of her brown hair worn free, her posture—all ordinary. But when my gaze came to her eyes, there was certainly a mystery there. A mystery that a thousand words could never tell but would have to be seen for itself. Each time I looked again I found a new mystery in her stare, something else I hadn't noticed before, which reeled me in deeper, beckoning me to who she really was. That for me is the beauty of the *Mona Lisa*. It's so much more than a painting.

The lady in the *Mona Lisa* painting was discovered to be Lisa del Giocondo, the wife of a silk merchant, and though she came from noble stock, her family was not particularly wealthy or well-off at the time of her marriage. Historians tell us that she was a good and faithful wife and well loved by her husband. A few years into her marriage, the painting of the *Mona Lisa* began by one of the most renowned painters in the history of man, Leonardo di Vinci.

Under French law, the *Mona Lisa* is deemed priceless. France prohibits sale of the painting as it belongs to the people of France; this also means it has "infinite value" (as a sale price cannot be agreed). Were this law to change for any reason enabling a sale, the painting would be worth billions of pounds—close to £1.5 billion today.

In the same way, our self-image is worth more than we could ever imagine.

In this chapter, we'll examine intimacy when it comes to ourselves. We'll explore the concept of seeing or knowing all of who we are, not just on a superficial level, but on a much deeper one. It's vital that we each examine our self-image and learn to appreciate who we are and how God created us. So we'll look at our journey of intimacy with God also.

Fine Lines, Layers and Cracks

The *Mona Lisa,* which was created starting in 1503, is now over five hundred years old. It has aged considerably and acquired cracks along the way. This is known in the art world as crackle or craquelure—a fine pattern that consequently forms on the surface of the paint layer. Humidity or temperature fluctuations cause little cracks in the painting, and to what extent this happens is down to the ingredients used, the quality of paint or the type of canvas, and of course, the passing of time.

In the same way, fine lines form on our faces through stretching and pushing. The fluctuations in rhythms, temperature, and passage of time enable these lines to occur naturally. Cracks reveal layers. A true portrait of our lives can only be depicted in layers, like layers of earth or soil, and when seasons change, this has an extraordinary effect on those layers. The certainty we have is that seasons will change; however, how well our soil adapts is down to many other factors.

Like the cracks on the *Mona Lisa* painting caused by temperature changes, humidity, and other environmental conditions, we also go through sometimes dry and parched land in the world and that causes cracks in our existence, but rather than allow them to destroy us, we allow them to add texture to the journey and define hope and beauty for the generations that follow.

Cracks in our world are undeniably a result of the numerous complex layers of individuality we each possess and how well we manage to harmonize them or disenfranchise them along our journey.

Our Self-awareness, Our Layers

Intimacy is derived from the Latin word *intimus,* which means "inner" or "innermost." The art of intimacy always begins with self. We learn to appreciate ourselves and others much more through making the right choices in exploring our innermost qualities. It helps us relate well on many different levels and build productive relationships.

When I was a little girl, I thought I knew a lot—about myself, about people, and about things in general. Now that I am older, I think what a lot of foolishness that was, but even the Good Book says that foolishness dwells in the heart of a child. Even foolishness has its purpose to serve, or else there would be none the wiser and certainly no need for developing self-awareness.

When we are younger, we tend to have a sense of invincibility, like we can do almost anything and have got all the time to do it. I think that is why we might try lots of things with less scepticism. We are also paradoxically far more susceptible to peer pressure. I think for a woman like myself, this happens because the lens of focus provided is sometimes very narrow, making us think we have very few options that ensure our wholeness or fulfilment or reason for existence, thereby restricting us and resulting in the accumulation of many veils rather than setting us free. As we hopefully get wiser, more aware, and more astute, the layers of who we have been labelled to be begin to peel back. Then, our invincibility changes our dependency, as what we depend upon becomes more concrete and solid, because what we now rely on is no longer external but internal.

We have many layers and, consequently, it takes time to know one another. When people work together, time is needed to understand each other to work better together. It's the same with a romantic relationship, with raising children, or in teaching students. A kind of symbiotic relationship needs to form, and this takes time and invested energy for a true unveiling to occur.

This unveiling doesn't only happen in relation to others; it happens in relation to yourself and how you create the right equilibrium in managing those different layers. Time is needed to get to know you.

Learning my layers has been such an interesting and sometimes uncomfortable part of my growth. Part of the discovery has been the thin line between self-conceit and self-consciousness. In between these two extremes is the precious zone of "self-awareness." As much as self-awareness is necessary in various dimensions of life, family, and society, it is a fundamental building block in learning ourselves.

Sometimes we veer more toward the self-conscious end of the scale and inhibit ourselves and expressions, ultimately hiding because we are afraid what people might think of us. Other times, we display an over-inflated opinion of ourselves as a false defence mechanism. Whether we do this consciously or not is part of really getting to know ourselves and balancing the layers.

Take some time right now to think of yourself and

your journey between self-conceit, self-consciousness, and self-awareness. It may vary depending on circumstance or the particular relationship in question. Where do you find yourself right now? Where would you like to be?

Growing up, I always loved to read and write. As far back as primary school, I recall writing interesting essays. In my primary school, the tradition was for the best essays written in the week to be read at school assembly in the mornings. One day, when I was about eight years old, mine was chosen. I was mortified because I was a shy little girl. I was so nervous reading aloud on the raised stage at the front of our assembly hall that day, making sure my book completely covered my face to obscure the sea of faces in front of me.

When the headteacher, whom we referred to as the principal, asked me a question about the story, I could not answer correctly. I was so choked up with emotion afterward because I felt embarrassed at being unable to answer the question. Furthermore, I was mortified at all the attention I was receiving, whether perceived as positive or negative. The subsequent essays I wrote were read by other children in my class because I simply refused to put myself through what I considered to be a grave and unnecessary ordeal. My state of self-consciousness had caused a disequilibrium, and a veil had been cast over something that really was attractive in itself—my love for writing.

I still can't really say precisely what caused me to be so self-conscious at that age; perhaps it was simply my shy nature, a layer that would erode with time.

Fast-forward many years later—I work at a nonprofit organisation, presenting and training operational managers and regional directors. Did that self-conscious little girl show up? Absolutely, but I pushed my self-consciousness aside to focus on the need. People needed the information I had; these managers were seeking knowledge that I could provide. My awareness of this need helped to create an equilibrium with meeting my objectives in this situation and managing what I thought people were thinking of me.

The lesson here is that I was once defined as "shy and timid," yet there was a depth, a layer to my vessel, that completely flawed that assertion. There was and is still an extroverted side to me, but that side is not always required. It has taken many experiences to realize its existence and to normalize our acquaintance.

In the process of "seeing into me" (in other words, getting to know myself), I have learned to become more self-aware and allow self-conceit and self-consciousness to fall away. I have learned as well to understand the places I am and how I can be most effective. This has taken time and experience.

My metaphoric fine lines are created from those experiences that have stretched me both positively and negatively, that have pushed me and sometimes pressed me. This is the evidence of things tested. Our fine lines are the evidence of things tested in the cause of our unique journey.

Fine lines left without moisture for long periods will result in cracks, but cracks do not always result in structural damage, particularly where our different layers are managed properly, where we are oiled and watered sufficiently.

We all have layers. Some of these layers are unknown to us yet perceived by others. Some are known to us and hidden from others. Some are known by us and others, and some I believe are still unknown to ourselves and the rest of the world.

Changing seasons are one of the main determinants to these layers being revealed or hidden away, being understood, and even being transformed or renewed. It is important that we are particularly discerning in changing seasons to see who and know who we are becoming or could potentially become. I have discovered it is not about how parched the experience gets but rather the assurance that water and oil will flow again to fill those cracks. The combination of these things influences the eternal design that eventually evolves on the canvas.

Intimacy with Our Painter

It would be remiss of anyone to speak of the *Mona Lisa* without mention of the painter himself. The *Mona Lisa*, along with the rest of Leonardo da Vinci's body of work, exemplifies his impeccable talent and genius. It is clear da Vinci was without rival in what he accomplished as a painter. In the same vein, it would be remiss of me to speak of the *Mona Lisa* without mentioning Leonardo da Vinci. It would also be remiss of me to speak of my self-image without speaking of God.

It is funny how little our trust is when it comes to God and the portrait he is painting with our lives, both individually and collectively.

There are many depths, many edges, and even heights to which the thoughts of the painter may wonder in search of the truth when he creates his painting. He will add layers that over time will be completely immersed in translating his imagination and bringing it to life. In this exchange, the painter-creator loses something momentarily in hope of a far greater reward, the painting. When we think of God as our Painter, His painting is you and me.

Painters like Leonardo da Vinci are intimate with their paintings. The time, energy, and thought they invest in their work leads to this intimacy. In the same way, our Painter, God, wants to be intimate with us. I cannot think of the word intimacy without thinking of the word "knowing." This term is used in the context of the Bible to describe the intimacy between a man and his wife: "Now the man Adam **knew** Eve his wife; and she conceived, and gave birth to Cain" (Genesis 4:1 AMP). Knowing is not just sexual; it is also used to describe emotional and cerebral interactions that hopefully lead to a productive, fruitful relationship.

In John 14:7 (AMP), Jesus said, "If you had really **known** me, you would also have **known** my father . . ." Obviously, sex is not implied here, but rather a connection that involves the spirit, mind, and heart. This is a connection that brings us into a deep knowledge of the Father.

Intimacy with or knowing another person means you dive into them, you press in. You are actively curious to discover who they are, what they are made of, what they can do and not do. It is an active search to discover and then become wrapped up in what you have discovered. Yes, to the point of distraction. The problem we find is that we are sometimes off getting distracted by other people instead of getting intimate enough with ourselves and God to that level of distraction.

The word "infinity" means limitless or endless in space, extent, or size; impossible to measure or calculate. Intimacy with ourselves and God is an infinite journey, one that you and anyone else who loves you will need to commit to unconditionally.

Deep Communion Diving into the Layers

There are many reasons why we may feel or have a deep connection with someone else. Maybe the connection is a result of our strengths, our gifts, our weaknesses, our hurts, or our vulnerabilities.

The word "vulnerable" is derived from the Latin noun *vulnus* ("wound"). The *Merriam-Webster Dictionary* says vulnerable has been "used figuratively to suggest a defencelessness against both physical and non-physical attacks." When we make ourselves vulnerable, this basically suggests a direct path or opening into a normally enclosed and protected area to avoid being hurt.

Sometimes, in order to gain trust or win over another, we make ourselves vulnerable. We choose to risk the possibility of hurt to demonstrate our stake in the relationship. This has the ability to disarm but inadvertently gives you an instantaneous advantage.

Getting to know yourself, others, and your Creator involves a deep communion. As part of the art of intimacy, let's look at three hallmarks of deep communion.

Vulnerability

We cannot really commune with anyone without being vulnerable in some way. The highest level of vulnerability was when Jesus exposed himself to be crucified on the cross.

Because of this act, He is the only one a believer can have the deepest level of communion with, and He alone can give us a true understanding of our self-image in that exchange. When the painter recreates his subject on a canvas, it isn't just a likeness he seeks to capture; he seeks to capture the vulnerable parts of his subject as well, the unique quirks and mannerisms that almost bring the painting to life. This is what our Creator seeks to achieve as He communes with us—to bring us to life completely.

Relationships require us to be vulnerable, and whether or not we realise we are doing it, we do open up ourselves in a bid to encourage trust and know the truth about the other person as well. This will not apply to love bombers or heartbreakers or swingers just looking for a short boost. I am referring to serious-minded people genuinely looking to build a good relationship or even cultivate a lifetime friendship or nourish a corporate relationship. All these different areas will still require some kind of exposure to gain trust, and we must be careful in choosing who we forge these relationships with.

When George Floyd was killed in the US in 2020 by a law-enforcement officer, the Black Lives Matter movement blew up across the world, highlighting a significant crack in our world today. A societal crack that exposed the construct of racism was again highlighted by this event. There were and continue to be many corporate organisations demonstrating more vulnerability by fostering working environments that enable a variety of lived experiences to be shared. We exist in a global village, with many different cultural backgrounds colliding on a more frequent basis than ever before. The corporate world is learning to make room for this by leading with more vulnerability and enabling that value to permeate the organisations they lead. This is a bid to build trust and encourage meaningful exchange with employees across various parts of the organisation and the communities they exist in. I have been involved in webinars and training sessions where individuals are called to share their lived experiences, and mentoring sessions often require this, too. The aim is to build trust and achieve a reasonable level of communion that allows genuine relationships to flourish. I have facilitated sessions where I shared my own lived experience of being locked down as a single mom in a pandemic. And I have gained a rich community of women who are not only mums but with whom I share many other interests and can call friends.

Vulnerability requires a conducive environment, and many times that needs to be intentionally created or sought out.

Patience

Understanding things sometimes can be difficult. People, places, culture, pain, loss, and even love can present a considerable level of difficulty. And sometimes understanding yourself can be difficult. It takes patience, process, and playback to be clear sometimes. Even then, it still may not be clear. I do not believe there is finality in uncovering the mystery of who we are because there isn't finality in uncovering where we have come from.

When we think about patience, we are often focused on the waiting aspect. Conversely, we could consider what we are doing when we are "not waiting patiently"—we are likely rushing, in a haste. Haste results in waste and rushing likely means you will miss some of the detail you are required to pay attention to in yourself or in a relationship, those golden nuggets that could save a huge argument from happening. Haste means you are likely not taking time to understand or appreciate your peculiarities and the different dimensions that make you whole and true. Haste means you may not be accepting of the present, so how will you know what needs to change so you can cultivate a better version of yourself for the future?

Also, as we grow in society, we have deep communion with social patterns and ways of life. Our family traditions and our education, for example, are aspects of life with which we have deep communion each day. This communion is so important because we need to understand the world around us.

In the Bible, we are told Jesus surrendered himself on the cross and was proclaimed Prince of Peace. Before this, though, He walked and worked with the same people He came to save. He went to parties with His disciples, visited the temple with them, taught crowds of people, and even had His fallout with the merchants who were selling wares in the temple. He communed with the people and in the society, experiencing many traditions, families, and ways of living, but never forsaking His own. He got to understand the people He would later lay down his life for, and it took a lot of patience knowing what He knew from the Father. There are many layers or facets to us as human beings, and Jesus needed to experience them fully before surrendering at the cross. He knew what it was to be a babe and then a boy and then a man; he knew what it was to be the apple of His mother's eye and scorned by the Romans. He knew what it was like to be taught and to teach. He knew love and He knew hate.

We also experience many of these situations and emotions in our lives. The pillar of patience helps us endure the rough patches with grace and look forward to the more pleasurable experiences with joy.

Repetition

Repetition implies that we keep at a particular act, pattern, or rhythm on a regular basis. It doesn't matter how many times we are told we are loved; we want to hear it again and again. I tell my son I love him regularly; it doesn't stop him from asking me every now and again if I love him. And why is it that no matter how many times we may render praises to God, we still need to keep at it? Why is there a need to regularly attend fellowship and be with our sisters and brothers? Even for those who are not Christian, they regularly gather to relate with one another. Why do we eat regularly? Why does a couple begin to feel distant without regular intercourse? These things are done to maintain and grow our communion.

The painter understands that this golden thread of communion needs to run through the portrait. In the same way these elements help hold the portrait together, they should also hold fast in every season of our lives as a golden acknowledgement that really confirms we are one.

What we also find in deep, genuine communion is water and oil for our journey, so that those dry patches can be endured far better, so that the strain on us is not unbearable, so that we have a place to exhale.

There are many movements across the world that speak on behalf of many different groups of people. These movements for many present water and oil. For each of these movements to flourish, someone has taken time to understand a group of people, has endured their pain, has been privileged to be blessed by their gifts or talents, and is committed to advocating for them—and it all started by being in relationship with them. That relationship is a healing process, a renewal and restoration that will permeate generations. As the cycle repeats itself, this is true communion.

When we consider the world as it is today, technological advancements have made it such that we can exist even more isolated. This pandemic of isolation is one of the reasons for debilitating mental health conditions and the reason we might experience or observe various states of inequality. Learning another person or culture, which could be learning their pain or limitation, reduces isolation. But simply "learning another" can many times be considered an inconvenience in our world today. Yet there are so many layers into which we can bring water and oil so that the cracks that exist in our society are healed and renewed or restored. When this happens there is true communion.

"Our portrait is already complete; it is already a masterpiece. It has been painted flawlessly by God, and all we are doing is walking the road of discovery and trusting that neither the hardships nor challenges we encounter will diminish what has already been destined for us, in us, or through us."

Rule and Reign

There is a saying that goes, "The apple does not fall far from the apple tree." The way a painter expects his art to be a masterpiece is akin to our Creator anticipating that we rule and reign in the places and seasons we find ourselves. Understanding how God wants us to rule is part of understanding our self-image and is part of intimacy.

Like kings, we were created to have dominion. Kings search things out. Kings are positioned to rule. Kings have a glorious inheritance.

> *"God said, Let Us [Father, Son, and Holy Spirit] make mankind in Our image, after Our likeness, and let them have complete authority over the fish of the sea, the birds of the air, the [tame] beasts, and over all of the earth, and over everything that creeps upon the earth."*—*Genesis 1:26 (AMPC)*

A king is expected to meet huge challenges head on. One of the reasons he is in that position, usually by virtue of the people, is because they believe he can make the right decisions in meeting those challenges for them. It is no coincidence that we are referred to as "kings," "queens," and "royalty" by God Himself. In the old days, a king was seasoned by many wars where he fought with his soldiers—consider King David and his many victories that led to many lands being conquered.

Metaphorically speaking, let us consider our own territories that God has predestined for us to claim on earth for His glory. He already knows we have what it takes to overcome those challenges. The story of King David illustrates this so well because he was anointed king many years before he ascended the throne of Israel. His life also shows repetition in his interactions with God. There was constant communion between David and God, even when things didn't go the way David expected.

The measure of a king extends beyond riches and wealth. It is weighed in wisdom, in people. As it says in Proverbs 14:28 (AMPC), "In a multitude of people is the king's glory, but in a lack of people is the prince's ruin."

The measure of a king is also weighed in land territory. Joshua 12 does a great job listing the names of kings and the land they occupied or had authority over. Only a king can give his land away, and he chooses a "royal subject" because that individual bears likeness to him in some way or is in agreement with him. Agreement could be in the fact that they have become subject to the king because they have been won over in a battle or war. Many such treaties existed in the Bible. A royal subject is usually related to the king, or the subject has proved himself to be of such value that the king chooses to give him responsibility or stewardship over his land.

Rulership is applied in so many different contexts, including work life, home life, community life, and education. To take authority over a situation, we must search it out; we must gain as much understanding of it as we can. We must go down low before we raise up high. When we try to understand things, we naturally assume a lower posture and we humble ourselves. We are extra cautious to gain clarity from the people and things we find around us.

We cannot speak of a king or royalty without reference to their majesty, authority, wealth, or the enormous influence they have. However, we also speak of their mercy and leniency, their kindness and steadfastness. In other words, we cannot speak of royalty without consideration of the things that make them so.

In a portrait of a person, such as the *Mona Lisa*, it is ensured that the person is the object of attention. The subject is the dominating feature of the portrait. We all have something or somewhere we are assigned to dominate, either by virtue of our gifts or of our talents, things that are quite naturally a part of who we are. These qualities are what usually dictate and design areas of dominance. Part of the journey is figuring out what these are for us personally.

God has placed those unique attributes in us so that He may be glorified. This is the art of intimacy, the Painter's ability expressed through you. The more we discover and lean into these unique attributes and trust how He wants us to use them, the more we experience a deep sense of wholeness and authority.

Glory

The concept of glory is often depicted as something we chase after, the reward after a long struggle or season of perseverance. Glory is what we lost in the garden of Eden. It is what was taken back from us when Adam and Eve disobeyed God, and it is what was restored when Jesus died on the cross and we accepted him. At that point, we agreed to share in His sufferings and His glory.

Glory is revelation. Sharing in the glory of God is essentially the revelation of who we are in Him.

For this reason, we must know God has always wanted us to share in His glory, or else He would never have sent His son. The glory was restored when Jesus came to die for us. This glory is infinite. God hid His glory from Moses because he considered that Moses would not be able to behold him.

That was part of a mystery.

> *"And God said, I will make all My goodness pass before you, and I will proclaim My name, The Lord, before you; for I will be gracious to whom I will be gracious, and will show mercy and loving-kindness on whom I will show mercy and loving-kindness. But, He said, You cannot see My face, for no man shall see Me and live. And the Lord said, Behold, there is a place beside Me, and you shall stand upon the rock, And while My glory passes by, I will put you in a cleft of the rock and cover you with My hand until I have passed by."* —Exodus 33:19–23 (AMPC)

Even God is cautious and careful in the way He reveals Himself to us, yet we are sometimes careless in revealing and sharing ourselves with others. We cannot really get a revelation of God without Jesus, and this is the reason Jesus was sent, because God desired so deeply that we would have this revelation of Him.

A revelation or what we could call a self-discovery journey is unnecessary if we think we already know everything there is to know about ourselves. And so it says in 1 Corinthians 13:12 (AMPC): "For now we are looking in a mirror that gives only a dim (blurred) reflection [of reality as in a riddle or enigma], but then [when perfection comes] we shall see in reality *and* face to face! Now I know in part (imperfectly), but then I shall know *and* understand fully *and* clearly, even in the same manner as I have been fully *and* clearly known *and* understood [by God]."

The beginning of seeing our true self is not about how precisely or entirely we do it, but in acknowledging at each stage of the journey that all that needs to be known is known, and that revelation will keep evolving as we forge forward onto greater things. It is an acceptance that we are changing as we step further into the light, not to be seen but to see. We are already fully seen and completely known by God, but our knowledge of Him is progressive.

There was a time when Moses could not look at God; in fact, he was ordered to hide in between the rocks so he would not be blinded. Yet now we know that Moses is in the presence of God beholding his glory constantly, because this was confirmed at the transfiguration of Jesus. Now Moses beholds the glory of God more precisely where once his form required him to hide from it.

Within this unfathomable light exists many and varied impressions, and even reflections, all within us. The brilliance of this light is shining and clear. As it says in Revelation

21:10–11 (AMPC), "Then in the Spirit He conveyed me away to a vast and lofty mountain and exhibited to me the holy (hallowed, consecrated) city of Jerusalem descending out of heaven from God, Clothed in God's glory [in all its splendour and radiance]. The lustre of it resembled a rare and most precious jewel, like jasper, shining clear as crystal."

Note the phrase "*in the Spirit, He conveyed me.*" This was obviously a deep spiritual experience that brought John, the author of the book of Revelation, to this realisation, or, if you like, this revelation.

We have all been created uniquely, and to get in touch with that uniqueness, there is a level of intimacy required with self, your mind, and your spirit.

Colours of Light

In order to see, we need light. Contrary to what we may see with our natural eyes, light comes with a multitude of colours. Every painting needs colour. Colours are necessary for creating a portrait even when it's just black on white, yet no one single image or self-portrait is ever meant to be the same.

We all emit our own unique light on this earth. That particular lustre you emit is unidentical to any other and yet completely recognisable in creation. This is why it is such a disappointment when we try to replicate the life of another, as if there is nothing unique about us. Comparing ourselves with others is actually a fear of being seen; it is a twisted attempt to hide ourselves and stay in the dark.

We shouldn't lose the essence of who we are in getting

along with people because that particular lustre is only found in us. We shouldn't let adaptability define us; we let it refine us. The word "adapt" means to make something suitable for a new use or purpose. The real question is this: Is the new use or modification meant for you? Is the new experience a space for your vessel? We all have our essence and purpose. If we were to change these every time a new season presented itself, we would rob ourselves of our authenticity and probably not do what it is we are primarily supposed to in the way we are supposed to. Our adaptability should refine our light—that is, make it better and brighter, not change it completely to make it what it isn't simply for the convenience of being in a new space that does not cultivate it effectively. So even when we must change, it should be considered carefully.

A huge part of being our unique self is reflecting our particular lustre, but if it is lost, so are we.

Beneath the Surface

Our self-image goes much deeper than the surface of things. What we know of it is constantly evolving as our knowledge of love keeps increasing and growing.

My journey has brought many self-revelations and snippets of me: downtrodden, insecure, gifted, misunderstood, down-to-earth, expectant, childlike, passionate, kind, unrelenting, gracious, adventurous. As in any portrait, along with the luminous aspects, there are also shadows between the lines. The benefit of assessing these different parts with humility and honesty is that we connect with light that leads us to truth.

Can you identify various self-revelations in your journey? What are some words you'd use to describe yourself or name yourself?

We cannot understand or discern the times appropriately if we do not assume the right posture of heart and mind to receive it. Assuming a ready posture in itself suggests that it is the right time, because it indicates obedience and an aversion for contradicting a truthful opinion of ourselves. What happens in this space is that God can reveal more about Himself. He lets you in a little deeper to experience even more intimacy with Him.

Oswald Chambers said, "The tiniest fragment of obedience and heaven opens and the profoundest truths of God are yours straight away. God will never reveal more truth about Himself until you have obeyed what you know already."

I once struggled with a sense of self-righteousness, but I could not see that until I was hurt by someone struggling with the same thing. This is a frequent occurrence in relationships today. People are attracted to others because of the same weaknesses they are struggling with. Instead of walking in freedom by assessing the truth, we breed many lies and concentrate on the weakness, making the relationship a tremulous one.

When I discovered the trap that I had literally laid for myself because of a lack of self-awareness, love began to speak to me. That love revealed more and gave specific instructions on how I needed to back out of those situations if I didn't want more damage. Love revealed that I could find comfort in who I was, that I needed to be my own best friend, and that I could heal my mind. Love revealed depths I never knew existed in me. It took me to my core where I experienced mercy, grace, and the truth—that I am the object of great love and affection, beloved. Never have I felt more entwined with my Maker as the times when I have fallen flat on my face and been genuinely repentant. In those moments, I stepped into a new dimension of my relationship with love. It always takes my breath away when I am reminded of the image He has of me and not the image that others would project on to me.

Crucible Moments

What I think of myself is searched out in the quiet, sometimes in the heated crucible moments no one else knows. There, indelible values are forged or reinforced. You can hear a lot in the quiet moments, and it is imperative that you are hearing the right things.

Crucible moments act as chisellers—scraping away any excess material to bring out the real and true sculpture. In some seasons, there will be people who act as chisellers—people in relationship with you who challenge you and sometimes surprisingly enable a better and strong version of you to emerge. Sometimes the circumstance itself is the chiseller. You might find yourself in financial distress or emotionally bankrupt, or you might find yourself in a new town with no one to call friend and no family close by, at least not physically. In some seasons, both the circumstance itself and the people act as chisellers. And those who close the door on you only serve to create the crucible moments that crystallise beautiful and true you.

Where I have been stuck long in places, akin to the nooks or crannies of the mountain I aspire to conquer, I was wrestling with things I had the misconception of thinking that I could do all by myself! This is a most human experience; we want to maintain control of the situation, but the truth is we have no more control of the situation than a pound of batter has in a heated oven. The pound of batter will rise as it is stimulated by high temperatures, and a furious reaction takes place in that oven with a single expected result.

The heat from the air in the oven is transferred from the atmosphere in the oven to the inside of the batter where a significant structural change takes place. As this structural change occurs, a fragrance is released. And if I were a sculpture, indeed there would be unwanted pieces of me flying across the place as my sculptor chiselled away to reveal something amazing.

In the Scripture, we are described as a perfume, a "fragrance" of Christ: "But thanks be to God, who always leads us in triumph in Christ, and through us spreads and makes evident everywhere the sweet fragrance of the knowledge of Him. For we are the sweet fragrance of Christ [which ascends] to God, [discernible both] among those who are being saved and among those who are perishing; to the latter one an aroma from death to death [a fatal, offensive odor], but to the other an aroma from life to life [a vital fragrance, living and fresh]. And who is adequate and sufficiently qualified for these things?" (2 Corinthians 2:15-16 AMP) "" (2 Corinthians 2:15–16 CEV).

The fragrance that goes up represents the burning of the unwanted coming from the sacrifices you make or things you deny yourself to be a better version of you. Some people might be happy about this happening to us, and some will not be happy about this because they prefer to keep colluding with the broken version of you that has no intention of being more or being all that it has been called to be. We find sometimes that our image is not stable because of the counsel we receive that is inconsistent with God's standards.

The painter's material is evidently critical to this process of painting his object. Many times what began as an exquisite canvas or paintbrush is corrupted by environmental conditions and unprecedented occurrences. This is where our own level of discernment proves useful in guiding us to making the right turns on the path before us as we remain sensitive to changing seasons.

"See into me," which simply translates as intimacy, presents the idea of seeing something for the first time as very ordinary, but that's only because what is within has not been explored or considered, yet it has infinite value.

The opportunity to discover can be an exciting one, more so when you are at the centre of that discovery process.

In this chapter, we have explored our self-image at a deeper level through a few concepts that enable us on the path of intimacy, including self-awareness, three hallmarks of deep communion—vulnerability, patience, and repetition—and rulership, glory, and crucible moments.

Self-discovery is a continuous process because we are always, I hope, growing and changing, becoming a better version of ourselves. We will never know everything we desire to know about ourselves on this side of eternity, but we can always be challenged to seek it out. There lies the magnificent mystery to us, or else we wouldn't need to be on a journey of continuous discovery, which in itself necessitates this "art of intimacy."

Yet our portrait is already complete; it is already a masterpiece. It has been painted flawlessly by God, and all we are doing is walking the road of discovery and trusting that neither the hardships nor challenges we encounter will diminish what has already been destined for us, in us, or through us.

Flawless Finish Pointers

- To truly see the unique image that you are, deep communion is required.
- The beginning of seeing yourself as you truly are is to accept that you are changing as you step further into the light, not to be seen but to see.
- We shouldn't lose the essence of who we are in getting along with people; that particular lustre is only found in us. We shouldn't let adaptability define us; we let it refine us.
- Our portrait is already complete; it is already a masterpiece. It has been painted flawlessly by God, and all we are doing is walking the road of discovery.

Small Group Discussion Questions

- How do you see yourself?
- What aspect of life make you feel well-nourished and why?
- What kinds of societal cracks have you witnessed around you lately?
- Which of the three pillars of deep communion is the one most regularly used in your life?
- Why do we need to vulnerable? With what kind of people and at what times could we be vulnerable? How can we learn from those experiences to love ourselves a bit more?
- Can you recount any experiences where you have naturally assumed a dominant role? How did this happen? Did it positively impact you or the people around you, and if so, how?
- Why do you think relationships can sometimes be hard? How do you practice self-awareness in your daily patterns?
- What parts of your image do you think reflect God's image?
- Why do you feel betrayed when things don't work out the way you expect them to in a relationship?
- Why might you suffer from the fear of being seen sometimes?
- Reflect on a crucible moment in your life.

Chapter Two

THE WRESTLE

Like diamonds found in the roughest terrains, many men and women like myself are forged in some of the roughest landscapes, but the belligerence of these environments has only served to bring out the very best in us. Wrestling with hardships has served in enabling us to identify with our core, anchoring us to what is stronger within us, and releasing our voices to be heard and echoed further and wider than we could have ever imagined.

There may be worse things than being the odd one out or the foreigner or even the rebel, but I don't think there is anything worse than not knowing who you are.

There are many things we may use to identify ourselves with in this world or in different seasons, and there are many layers to us that heighten the stakes in our wrestling.

I am the third-born female child of a Nigerian man

and a Nigerian woman. My father is a surgeon, and my mother was a secretary who later studied law after her children were grown. I was married to the father of my child, but I am now legally divorced. I am currently a single parent. I am employed. I am a Christian. I live in the United Kingdom. I have been broke and unemployed, physically abused and discriminated against. I have felt like an outcast in more ways than one—at times I have felt unqualified, unsuitable, unwanted, incapable, unseen, and sometimes afraid. I was afraid because underneath all one might see my deep-rooted fear that somehow, I wasn't enough, and I wanted to prove that I was. Sometimes you find that you have absolutely nothing to prove—that your mere existence is simply enough proof that you are worth it.

I have been challenged and I have been reborn.

Make of that what you will.

There is a term trending in the media, society, and the corporate world: intersectionality. Intersectionality can be defined as "the interconnected nature of social categorizations such as race, class, and gender as they apply to a given individual or group, regarded as creating overlapping and interdependent systems of discrimination or disadvantage." This term is our attempt to join up and acknowledge all aspects of who we are or what we identify with, the parts that perhaps have been left unappreciated, maybe discriminated against, or left us feeling disadvantaged in some respect. Alternatively, they could be those parts that have enabled us to realise an identity unique to us or those we have come from that have indeed strengthened us.

Yet our social, physical, and even geographical dissections do not have the ability to encompass all of who we are. While this may be a liberating term, simply referring to me as a Christian or a single parent could never fully encompass all that I am or the many forms of discrimination, oppression, exclusion, or seclusion I might have experienced, even those self-imposed.

We might find it alarming when we discover these precious parts of ourselves and try on our own to make sense of each of them as we are confronted by the labels and tags the world might put on us.

Am I black? Exactly how black is black? Am I a Mucubal-nomadic-mother-black, or am I a single-male-American-Princeton-University-graduate-black?

Am I too young? How young is too young, if in reality, it's simply a conditioning of the mind?

Am I religious? When perhaps I might not profess to have a religion or follow any religious rituals regularly, but rather have a fate, a belief system, and a spiritual leader?

Am I single? As if singleness is condemnation to social exclusion rather than a celebration and fundamental part of my growth journey.

Am I there yet? When the truth is we never really get there; we are all sojourning, each believing for the best out of our individual paths, yet society expects certain boxes to have been ticked off at particular points in life.

Am I a parent? When in reality, we are all parents in some form or another as someone somewhere is looking up to us for guidance and correction.

Perhaps there are things you, too, have wrestled with.

What labels or tags have other people, situations, or society put on you? Have you wrestled with them?

All these experiences and tags or labels presumably will have points on an invisible scale somewhere we might choose to identify with, but none of this can be tangibly measured without really knowing an individual. There is neither a wrong nor right end of the scale to be on. The scale just is, same as we just are.

An age, a job, a marital status, a financial status, a religious status, a season of change—whatever a condition or label may look like, it does give birth to a wrestle with our image in some way. Sometimes it is short-lived and fleeting, and other times it could result in a major life crisis. All these contribute to our self-image and the different conjectures we have and certainly the final outcome. All these contribute to the nature and intensity of the wrestle.

A Fruit-Bearing Image

When we consider our fruitfulness as human beings, this has sometimes been stripped down to biological productivity. In many societies, increase or multiplication traditionally may be narrowed down to having biological children. However, when we consider the lives of people like Walt Disney, Martin Luther King Jr., Oprah Winfrey, and Mother Teresa, we understand procreation is beyond the physical womb. We have many sons and daughters through other means in this world because we all carry a womb that cannot be physically seen. Martin Luther King Jr. had biological children, yet it is the voice of his spiritual child that rings loudest today, even though he has been physically dead for fifty-five years. Oprah Winfrey has no biological children, yet her spiritual children are well known across the globe today, through many forums including film, books, schools, and other media platforms.

I am a single parent. Yet there are many other parts of me that bear fruit in the world, and these all present their own challenge.

While being a parent is so rewarding, it is also the most demanding call on my life. In addition, I happen to be raising a child in a community with few family connections, a community where I am quite possibly considered the foreigner or the outsider. The demands on me as a parent do not change because of my location or vocation; they remain the same and this will stretch any person significantly. Sometimes I have been so stretched to the point of feeling crippled, but the minute the season changes, it's obvious how much more elasticity has been ingrained in my thinking and my doing. Something new and expansive was cultivated in the wrestle.

When we learn to hang in there and refuse to give in to perfectionist tendencies, we will eventually find that we can run a little faster, go a little longer, and breathe a lot deeper. By leaning away from perfectionist tendencies, we open our hearts to receive what grace has for us and we find amazing things in the most unusual places and in relationships.

What we see come forth from the wrestle could potentially be an enormous amount of good fruit that actually feeds many around us, that nourishes us in our current circumstance and even future ones. While the seasons of wrestling and fruit-bearing may be separate, we can be sure one comes after another. Determination of the fruit is driven by what you choose to do in the wrestling moments.

I have lived in England for almost fifteen years, and I represent the black ethnic minority by virtue of my African heritage. This has surprisingly come with its own pressures, expectations, and sadly, discriminations, most of which I did not understand for a while. Within Nigeria, my country of origin, I identify with a particular minority group, the Efiks. This is my native tribe, and many tribal discriminations exist across the Nigerian geography as well. These tribal discriminations are not about colour; nevertheless, they do exist and sometimes could have detrimental outcomes within both the social and political scene. This confirms that as humans we almost always seem to find some level at which to discriminate against another, discriminate against ourselves, and disqualify ourselves before we have even begun the race.

I am a Christian living and working in a diverse community and corporate environment. That also has come with its share of prejudice, and often my standards do not align with those in the different arenas of life I find myself. This can be uncomfortable sometimes. Still, no matter how uncomfortable I get, it is my fate that grounds me. It is my belief system and a deeply rooted aspect of my core. It is what activates the light at the end of a really dark tunnel.

At one point, I was unemployed and living alone in a council flat while I cared for my newborn child. Those were peculiar years in my life. I want to call them hidden, but the truth is I was seen; however, I wasn't saying much about what I was going through. Perhaps I didn't think it was necessary since I was already talking to God about it. His voice was so clear to me in that season, and maybe this was because the voices of so many others had been silenced with my separation. God was so very tangible to me as I walked in and out of every room. He and I played an interesting duet in that season of my life.

In that season, I learned to better recognise His voice, gentle yet strong, and it has kept growing stronger even in the seasons when I have not felt Him as close. Although I had previously known God to some degree, at that time of my life, I found myself in uncharted territory. I was being forced to write a script that I had never been taught to write, nor was it one I had intended for my life. The sensations and feelings and sense of being I experienced were very different. I know now it was because He was revealing a different dimension of Himself to me. He was taking me further into places where I would permit fewer restrictions on my faith, and I found I stared less at myself and more at Him as each day unravelled.

One thing I discovered in my season of wrestling through heartbreak is that the truest, purest desire of any human being is to be known. We were created for that level of communion whether we realise it or not. This desire, placed right inside our hearts before we were fully woven, is something to be searched out, not hidden. The time for us to be completely known is not necessarily a privilege we own and that is what frustrates us sometimes. That's where most of our mistakes are made—we try to run ahead or lag behind. Sometimes the wrestle is simply finding that sweet spot of communion again with the one who understands it all even when we don't. Sometimes the wrestle is simply our own out-of-balance life asking us to stop and listen or stop and see.

The more I focussed on listening to my inner voice, the stronger I became.

Many of the struggles we have are about these different aspects of who we think we are. Much of the travail we experience in society and in the world are exaggerated in changing seasons or when we leave old territory for new territory. It is important to be conscious of this so we do not mistake every wrestle as an indication of a fault or shortcoming on our path.

What Does It Mean to Wrestle?

My personal struggles and seasons of wrestling have meant that I confront notions about myself or the ways of the world that are at odds with what my mind and heart have already accepted to be true. A wrestle occurs when there is contention, opposition, or conflict of some kind. Sometimes this happens within us, and it might mean you have reached a crossroads that requires you to see things differently or accept things you have refused to accept in the past, in order for you to—I hope—not simply move forward but upward. This process is almost like the seed buried that has finally made its way out of the ground in plant form. It is only then that the original seed can further develop structures and systems for bearing fruit, which it was ultimately planted for.

In each example of my personal wrestles, there were situations presented by the world and my circumstances that brought up many questions that could only have been answered by my Creator. As I gave Him space to provide the answers, I learned to trust more and more the incorruptible gifts He had put in me. I faced the wrestle of whether I was enough. The wrestle of feeling rejected. The wrestle of seeming different by colour or culture or aspiration. The wrestle of the single-parent syndrome. But those were the exact moments needed for the stirring so a new consciousness could emerge, so I could see He had not allowed them so I would go down, but rather that I would be carried up in the knowledge of how uniquely He had created me even for my trials.

If anyone ever tells you they have never wrestled with themselves, they lie.

The world is running on a broken rhythm and only one being can alleviate our suffering from within. The wrestle we experience is not unique to our generation. Men and women from ancient times have experienced this too. Jacob from the Bible was such a man who found himself wrestling, and I believe he was trying to find himself as he approached a crossroads in his own life.

According to the book of Genesis, Jacob goes through an intense wrestle just as he is about to meet his brother Esau, whom he had wronged and had not seen for many years. Since seeing his brother last, Jacob had become a man of great means and authority over his extensive household, yet he was a man fearful of meeting his brother again— indeed a paradox.

"Winning doesn't always mean you got the upper hand. Sometimes it simply means you got to understand the greater course and flow in that direction."

We sometimes chase wealth, fame, or accolades so that we become immune to dread and fear, so that our wealth will protect us. Yet we find in Jacob's case, his wealth did nothing to alleviate his fears. Jacob did not need anything from his brother except, perhaps, forgiveness. However, this man of enormous wealth and status among his family and people wrestled within himself. He left behind the home of his father-in-law and was sojourning back to a place he had left in a hurry because he had done someone wrong. Deep inside, Jacob was a man struggling with guilt about decisions he had made in his lifetime. It doesn't say so plainly in the Bible, but think about it—if you had by trickery taken something from someone you love, your conscience would surely chastise you. It doesn't matter how many years ago it happened or how much richer you were when you finally had to face the person—even more so if the person was once like a brother or sister to you.

The story says that in the middle of the night, Jacob wrestled with God. Isn't that the same as when we sit and tussle with the thoughts in our own mind, in prayer, in meditation, in hope and faith that things could be clearer and perhaps different?

Our mind becomes this oven of conjectures, and if we do not maintain the right temperatures while those conjectures cook, we could end up with a burnt offering that isn't acceptable to God.

Jacob's wrestle, however, was not just about what had happened with his brother—that is, his past. It was about what would happen in his future. He wanted to know that his future was secure in this land he was returning to. Going back to his source was an important exercise. I believe there were a few things Jacob had to accomplish in his wrestling, with the understanding that he would not be wrestling every single moment of his life, and with the knowledge that the wrestle was also a confirmation of an important juncture in his journey.

Having to wrestle does not mean you spend all of your life doing so. The process of wrestling is essentially part of an awakening. In this part of the journey, you reach deeper into who you are.

What can we learn from Jacob's wrestling? Let's look at six points.

- Jacob understood there was more to be done despite what he had achieved already, and it definitely wasn't just about the material things. He wanted the guilt lifted off him, forgiveness from his brother, and safety for his children. For you it might be the same. Or maybe it means extending kindness to people you have never thought to extend kindness to before and finding a new sense of purpose in doing that, a new venture that invigorates you and stirs your passion.

- Jacob approached his moment of wrestling by getting rid of excess weight and clutter. He basically sent his family and servants away. (He asked some to go ahead of him. While this was strategic, it was also necessary so he would have fewer distractions in his quiet deliberations.) He threw off some weight so he could get down to the business of clearing his mind. He needed to wholly disconnect from past patterns and mindsets that had created false and wrong behaviours. Usually, when there is a wrestle, we are holding on to things we should not be holding on to. Many things could weigh us down in life that really have little or no bearing on what we are about—our age, sex, country, marital status, the number of children we have. Think about what might be holding you down. Jacob pushed all of this aside in his wrestle, even the fact that he was merely a man wrestling with a supreme being. That is a warrior mindset. When we wrestle with this kind of mindset, there is only one outcome we expect—Glory.

- Jacob knew forgiveness was paramount in this situation, but he didn't know if he would receive it from his brother. From Esau's behaviour when they eventually met, it seems clear to me he had already forgiven his brother before they met. Jacob just didn't know. Deal with the guilt-tripping, please. If you have wronged someone, go apologise, and if someone requires your forgiveness, give it to them and let them know—you could save them a lot of heartache. There is a big difference in giving a person forgiveness and enabling them to treat you the same way again. Sometimes even in forgiving there needs to be separation so that the other party understands certain behaviours are not permissible, and if they really love you, they will adhere to your boundaries.

- Our determination is akin to our faith; it is our will. It is like saying to our will, "There is a way so find it." That's determination. Not giving up. No going down. This was the posture Jacob assumed in his conversation with God that night.

- Achieve mastery of something or someone. Prior to the actual wrestling event, Jacob spent time in a different environment than the one he grew up in. He learned a new trade from his father-in-law, and he mastered that trade to the point of becoming a lot more business-savvy than his father-in-law. He truly cultivated what he had been given.

  It makes me think of all the things we might be a part of before we arrive at those points where we wrestle, those transitory points, those opportunities for the new to be released. These moments, new as they might be, are still banking on investments you have already made. We must not take for granted our present simply because it is not where we think we should be or where we want to be, because they all add up to creating this amazing portrait for each of our lives. Whether we find ourselves representing a specific group or generation or experience—it all adds up to enriching us and we must never take it for granted.

- Jacob eventually accepted his weakness and yielded to strength that is unending. By doing this, his own strength became unending. Weakness is something we as humans do not like to associate with, yet it presents an opportunity. Even when we need to give up on things or let go, God can do what is only possible with His divine grace.

These words resonant much with the wrestling moments of life, a reminder not to give up. It acknowledges that living is fighting for the best version of ourselves. It speaks of fear that lingers in the dark and hope alive in the light—either could dictate the terms by which we exist. We activate the power of choice and enable the function of freedom. And sometimes there will be a wrestle.

So Missed

Solo and down in a pit,
Made to grasp at black space in order to find a way.
But there is nowhere to go in a pit.
The circular walls seem to close in
And above looms a foreign light, it's much safer in the pit,
you say.

Made to think all that exists is you and this dark empty place.
Your knees, they buckle at the slightest sound,
Your ignorance heightens your fear.
Despondence denies you any sense of care.
You do not know why or where you are.

The fear cripples you,
. . . since you let it sip through the dark cracks.
Dark cracks you allowed to infest your once light-flooded room.
Cracks that dared to encroach because your eyes roamed from
their own business.
Or was it your business?

Still your way can be found again,

Your light can be found yet again and then again.
Because no distance needs to be covered to attain it.
It is enveloped in the crevice of your wounded but still beating
heart.
Trust it.

In its perfect existence
Fear becomes insecure.
And insecurities become fearful men.
And that dark pit,
Oh! That dark, shoddy pit.
Suddenly fills up with bubbly goodness,
You are lifted by an overwhelming fragrance of peace
And now project an attractiveness that you alone can release.

It's inside, let it out,
Let your gorgeous glitter dust the world around
And let the world reply, "You have been so missed."

Our humanity has many broken aspects to it, and part of this is the struggle we have today in fully accessing who we are in the world. It is often said that "time heals all wounds," but in reality, time could pass without any healing happening or anything changing because we haven't personally done the work within ourselves to usher in the healing.

Every single one of us has at some point in our lives lost something—and sometimes the thing we lose is a sense of our identity. There is nothing lost that cannot be found, but there are some things that best remain lost because in losing them you gain so much more.

Reimaging

With losing things, there is always the great opportunity to replace them or even restate their purpose. It's such an exciting prospect to start something new and afresh. Like a blank canvas ready to have some coloured paint splashed all over it! With the right structures, tools, and belief system in place, a wonderful painting can emerge, a new beginning. Whatever the season you are in, it is possible to see differently and, yes, be different.

I spent a lot of time in that council flat mediating on the word and the truth. I remember I had the walls of my bedroom splashed with memorable verses so as I woke in the morning, they stared back at me. I had each of those cards signed "From your Father." I needed to know the truth so desperately because the world had fed me a lie and I had choked on it.

Reinventing

So maybe you aren't happy with who you have become. When this happens, we have a mind that can choose to change. We have the power to change it. If this is true, being connected to empty vessels or vessels with content that poison ours is dangerous for our self-image. In such situations, it is hard for us to really own our identity. Vessels that do not carry content suitable for our journey will often have a problem respecting our boundaries or having regard for our values. This will impede reinventing, reclaiming, or reimaging ourselves.

There is definitely power in simply changing your associations as you claim your identity. Some might say we are only as strong as our connections.

There are so many areas in my life right now where I know I am not as self-sufficient or even as confident as I was when I was much younger. Much of this is the result of where I placed my confidence and what or who I thought would make me self-sufficient. Now I know I have a perfected strength on the inside and this is without limit because I decided one night in the middle of a quiet council flat to move aside and let God do His thing as I was sitting in what I considered to be an atomic mess.

In all of this, through all the wrestle, I have come to know one thing is sure—all my layers, all my parts, all my seasons, all my uniqueness is loved, wanted, and enough. I am beloved. I am wanted. I am most certainly enough.

In this chapter, we have examined what it means to wrestle using both my personal life example and those of Jacob from the Bible. No one truly lives life without some kind of wrestle or struggle being presented to them. What these moments do is test us and urge us to go even deeper into ourselves to find what is perhaps constant and unchanging. Going a step further, it helps us appreciate the potential of what could be birthed from those wrestling moments or struggles with our image.

We have explored our self-image in parallel with fruit-bearing, reimaging, and reinventing of the self-image. These concepts are important to understand because there is always a by-product from our moments of wrestling. The desire is that what is produced is good and worthy of the beautiful image God has of you despite how tremulous the circumstance or situation creating the wrestle might be.

Many of us don't handle conflict or confrontation well. A good way of improving on this is by learning to wrestle well within ourselves so that we not only win more of those conflicts on the outside knowing who our source is, but also learn to lose with grace and without a dislocated limb like Jacob did.

The wrestle should give us hope that we can reimagine ourselves; we can discover or rediscover ourselves even when we are dissatisfied with who we have become.

Let's approach the wrestle with faith and not fear, with hope and not despondence, with light and not darkness. No matter how different we are or how varied our struggles may be, there is still huge potential to bear good fruit when we submit to the right spirit.

Flawless Finish Pointers

- There may be worse things than being the odd one out or the foreigner or even the rebel, but I don't think there is anything worse than not knowing who you are.
- The process of wrestling is actually part of an awakening. It's part of the journey so you reach deeper into who you are.
- Self-discovery does require some horsepower, some relentlessness, that attitude that says I won't go down.
- To deny yourself is to deny the world of you.

- Every season of life presents a different wrestle that could potentially take you deeper into who you are (very excitingly who you could be).
- Winning doesn't always mean you got the upper hand. Sometimes it simply means you got to understand the greater course and flow in that direction.

Small Group Discussion Questions

- What are those aspects of your self-image you have wrestled with and why?
- How have you affirmed yourself in those seasons of change?
- On the outside, everything could look perfect, but inside there is still a question: How do I really fit in this big picture—where is my territory?
- When last did you declutter? What did you do and how did you feel afterward?
- Have you tried to master any new skills or habits?
- What associations strengthen you? What associations weaken you? Why?
- Have you ever felt completely eclipsed at any time in your life? What did that feel like? How did you navigate that season? Who were your closest confidants, if any?

Chapter Three

OWNING MY IDENTITY

The whole premise of taking time to search something out or understand something is with the hope that we find something of value. In our case, as far as the Painter is concerned, our portrait is complete, and in completing the portrait, He has confirmed all of our value. The task left is for us to fiercely own the identity.

When we own something, it isn't enough to say it belongs to us and it isn't enough to be in possession of papers that give us claim to it. It is imperative that if something truly belongs to us, we use it and cultivate it, and by so doing we really put our stamp on it.

As much as ownership requires use, it also requires preservation. This means our identity portfolio carries risks.

The deeper the authenticity of the identity we claim, the higher the risks. Maybe this is why it is so hard for many of us to truly own our true identity, our authentic self, because in stepping out of the familiar—not simply that which is unfamiliar to us but also to everyone else—we potentially blaze a new trail, and we bring new light. This is not always welcome, and it certainly isn't easy to do.

Belief is one of those indelible qualities that have kept me going on my journey, and that belief was many times spurred by who I was hearing—the people speaking into my life, the words I was speaking to myself, the things I allowed to entertain me. We all have to believe in something, and the starting point is in ourselves.

What Is an Identity?

We base our identity on many aspects of life—country, language, culture, age, marital status, parental status, employment, relationship status, and the list goes on. These things barely scratch the surface of who we really are, though. For example, many ancestry findings suggest people who are living in certain parts of the world today migrated from an entirely different part of the world years ago. What does that really say about the places and traditions we choose to tie ourselves to here on earth?

Having said that, I love to identify with my African heritage and culture. Like anything else, it has its amazing bits and its not so amazing bits.

You might already be thinking about aspects of your life that contribute to your identity. Or if not, begin to think about them now. Consider the path this unique identity has put you on or what it has given you access to. There are many aspects of life that you might have been privileged to experience because of these defining elements of your identity, and it is important to know them and understand them as much as you can.

One of my favourite sensations is the feeling of my kinky hair between my fingertips. Weird, I know! It's funny how some of the things that bring us the deepest sense of comfort are the same things that cause the same measure of discomfort for others. I grew up as a young girl in Nigeria who enjoyed braiding her hair every now and again, wearing African print (Ankara) attires, dancing to Nigerian music, eating native delicacies, and watching masquerade festivities during the Christmas season. I have many fond memories attached to these aspects of Nigerian life. I have many memories which have nothing to do with my Nigerian culture but which I remain fiercely loyal to, no matter where I am or the condition in which I find myself. What I identify with most is what I love most, and sometimes it isn't the Nigerian factor. But I still cultivate this identity, and using it means that I have laid a claim on it.

I was born into a Christian family; I didn't have to choose this religion like some have. A Christian is deemed to be a follower of Christ. What I have realised along the way is that my religion and my relationship with the person Christ are two separate things. However, they are not mutually exclusive—in that I cannot say I am one of these without being the other. This identity of Christian cannot completely be claimed without the relationship with the pioneer of the Christian faith. Everything I get out of the religion is secondhand knowledge. While this might be useful, it does not totally build conviction nor sustain my belief, and the benefits of an authentic relationship with Him are not fully awarded nor experienced.

I haven't always had the relationship I now have with Christ; it has taken a lot of stumbling and groping to get to where I am now. There are some places, however, I completely refuse to go back to, behaviours and patterns that would disrupt the sweet spot I have found in Him. I could have only discovered this by intentionally investing in time to know Him and not simply conforming to religious rituals and traditions that sometimes breed legalism and stifle deep and meaningful relationships.

Seeing the Value in Ourselves

As humans, we instinctively desire to lay claims on things that add value to our lives. By seeing the value in ourselves, we build vigour to own our identity and grow to love it and truly appreciate the value it brings.

When I was in primary school, we played a game called "tug of war" quite often at breaktime or during sport events. As the name implies, it is quite a physical game. It requires two teams, each with a lead. At the start of the game, the leaders choose their teammates from the group of participants one at a time. Once this was done and each side had equal numbers (usually), each team stood in a straight line on opposite sides of a straight line drawn on the floor, with every single person holding on to a rope that ran from one end of one group to the other end of the other group.

The aim of the game was to see which team could pull the other over the line separating the two teams. With this aim in mind, the leaders handpicked their team members based on how powerful they thought they would be—how much strength they brought. If they looked strong enough or quick on their feet, they were on board. There was also consideration of their track record of success in this game. Physically small people tended to remain unpicked till last. We played this game often in school, so we knew the strong players from experience, not just sight.

While the leaders were picking, I remember some who had been picked would start bragging about others who were still waiting to be picked so that their team leader would take them quickly before the other team selected them.

Just like the leaders saw potential in others waiting to be picked, Christ saw value in me. Before I thought to be on Team Christ, He chose me because there was something in me that I hadn't yet seen in myself. He knew already what was valuable about me that often the natural eye does not. His affirmation birthed a belief in my true identity, and that identity is the most important aspect of me.

When we are inspired to use something or be around someone, it's because it or they have been a source of inspiration. Inspiration is the breeding ground for a higher level of freedom. I have been privileged to have a few mentors in my career and personal life, and what I have discovered is their ability to enable me to see beyond the present, beyond the now, to contemplate things I never would have before. It is just the most amazing feeling when you could so easily be bugged now with the present challenges or difficulties. This is what we do when we claim our identity: we begin working things out we may not yet see in the present. When we have assumed an identity that isn't our own and we seek the right one, inspiration goes a long way in helping us claim that.

A healthy mind doesn't freely give anything or anyone full access to influence their choices until there is proof of who or what they say they are. It is a natural thing to seek this kind of proof, yet it might not always come in the package we expect.

My first true acknowledgement of who God was to me was His gentleness with me. He proved Himself the gentle lover of my soul and a husband like none I have ever known of or experienced on this earth. In Him, I found my identity as beloved, wanted, and beautiful. There are many harsh realities that have laced my life, but his gentle hand was always there to reposition me and steer me right even when I didn't know what to do.

Many circumstances may leave us feeling like we have no one, or feeling rejected or unwanted, and at the same time unable to really articulate what we feel. Yet there is one who does not need you to speak because He knows your heart. His character of gentleness says, "I will love you through that deplorable situation. When you are ready to speak, I will listen. If all you have are your tears right now, I will sit here with you and hold you and breathe my light into you so you may glow again. Every step you take with me, I promise to protect and provide." Over and over, He proved this to me, and my assurance and confidence in His character grew. I felt good knowing He was sincere, true, and dependable.

Maybe you have wondered about God. Is He real? Does

He hear me? Does He see me? Maybe you could consider what relating with Him has been like. Consider the quiet contemplations you have and the thoughts that come back to you. What does a good relationship with Him look like? Is it a prayer in the morning or before you go to bed at night? Meditation of a Bible verse or listening to a podcast about Him? Maybe even talking to your friends about Him?

It wasn't impossible to have an identity while misplacing God in my life, but it was impossible to have my true identity and true self-image confirmed without Him. On this discovery journey of our value, our true image, it is important that we discover His value so we can fully and truly know ours.

Laying Claim

Your Words

Every self-affirming word you speak is a stake in the ground laying claim to your territory, yet even after you have put the stake in the ground, you still have to build fences around the land to confirm the boundaries to both you and the rest of the world. Your identity is akin to a boundary line you are setting, telling people what they could find within your territory if you permitted them entry or association of some sort.

Many of us have declarations we make on a daily basis. I like to think of my declarations as a personal creed I make to myself, to remind myself of who I am and what I am about in this world. I also think the declarative words needs to be rendered with a health warning because there is a thinking pattern that needs to accompany the words we speak. It isn't enough to say who we are; we must activate that person by acting in accordance with the words we have spoken. It is almost impossible to do this if toxic patterns, false beliefs, and lies planted through our life journey dominate our mind. Many such toxic patterns or false beliefs happened in our childhood years because our minds are so malleable then—like a sponge soaking in everything.

Our formative years exist in a learning environment. Some of the patterns cultivated are toxic patterns from false beliefs, and these take root and play over and over again in the mind. The cycle of repetition creates a pattern and essentially a behaviour. This can be referred to as our own internal system of working, and it's how our value is often cultivated.

For words to carry the required weight of integrity, it is crucial for toxic patterns to be broken to clear the way for the healthy patterns that reinforce who you are saying you are. Without this, you are just spewing out words.

Dr. Henry Cloud and Dr. Jon Townsend write in the book *Boundaries* that "your words let people know where you stand and thus give them a sense of the 'edges' that help identify you." And the Bible says in the beginning was the Word. Before anything was, the Word existed. Our 'Father's Word carried this ability to call things out of nothing, and since we are his offspring, so should our words. In order for these words to be effective, we need to purge our value system. Without the Word, nothing could have existed. Without your words, what is there to claim and own? Without your words, how does one begin to form a portrait of you? As 1 Peter 1:25 (AMPC) says, "But the Word of the Lord (divine instruction, the Gospel) endures forever."

The ultimate claim on identity was Jesus the risen Christ. He died, but in order to fully claim his title as risen King, he reappeared to his disciples in the flesh and confirmed His kingship and their redemption through Him. By reappearing in the flesh, He was demonstrating that He was the way "to life," the truth "for life," and ultimately, *the* life. He backed up His words with actions.

Conversely, there are seasons where there is no need for words. There are seasons when the most value we add is by being silent. In university, I once sat with a friend who was going through a rough patch. She had been ostracised by friends and was feeling really low. In all honesty, I didn't even know how she felt. I just knew I needed to be with her. While I was there, I apparently didn't say much.

Fast-forward almost twenty years later, and she tells me I did her a great service in a jacked-up season of her life. I could not even recall the precise moment she was referring to, if I am honest. Yet all she needed was my presence. I say this to remind us of the truth that our presence carries enormous value, and we may never know how much it means to the people around us, the people we love, the people we casually come in contact with. Our value sometimes may seem passive, but in those moments, it is doing its greatest work; it is actually in those moments or seasons that we are most effective.

Our quiet contemplations can be just as powerful as our words. A big part of refining our language, our words, is the effectiveness of our thoughts. I would urge you to consider intentionally the thoughts you have of yourself and your circumstance. What is the narrative flowing from there? Is it life-giving and inspiring? Does it have the potential to give life or cause death? Consider whether you need to change your thoughts so that they edify, because the minute you speak them, you have released power that could be confirming something about you.

Your Patterns

Whether we realize it or not, we have patterns that are created by our thought life. As Proverbs 23:7 (AMPC) says, "For as he thinks in his heart, so is he . . ." Whatever we are thinking on will eventually manifest itself in our lives through joy, fear, anger, you name it.

Research shows that our minds can have multi-perspectives so we can see things from different angles, and we have the ability to choose because we have been given free will. The more our mind identifies with a particular thought, the stronger that path becomes in our minds, like a bulldozer blazing a trail that will be travelled over and over again for as long as we allow the thought to play over in our brains. Where thoughts are good and righteous, it is to our benefit and the benefit of the world around us. And where they are toxic, the result is a debilitating one.

If our light is to shine brighter and brighter, our choices need to improve over and over, reflective of the Father of Light.

The root of a thought is just as important as the beginning of a road (journey). To truly identify whether a path is valid in our minds, we need to give sufficient thinking time or reflection time so toxic thought patterns do not evolve.

Blaise Pascal said, "Clarity of mind means clarity of passion, too; this is why a great and clear mind loves ardently and sees distinctly what it loves." If we are to be the city of light God says we are, we must see Him in everything we do and that starts with our thinking!

When we have the right pathways, they enable the right connections for us to facilitate our personal development, growth, and prosperity. Sometimes it is hard to imagine all of our prosperity is down to something as simple as a thought! Yet it is!

Your Voice

While I was writing this book, a friend asked me about the meaning of voice. Up until that point, I had never thought to actually define it in the context of my writing or my podcast. This is what I said, and I hope it rings true for you as well.

Voice is basically the essence of who we are. And that sound is echoed in what we do, who we love, what we are passionate about. While our voice can be audible, it is more strongly demonstrated in our actions and lifestyle, the causes we are endeared to. We find it by finding things we are passionate about and advocating for them mainly in the ways we speak, but also in our actions.

One of the things that makes our self-image truly authentic is the sound of our voice, the manner in which we speak, the conviction assigned to our repertoire, the texture of it, its particular vibration and effect.

Some of us need to find our voice on the premise that we

never knew what it sounded like anyway because we never had one. On the other hand, some of us need to find our voice on the premise that we had one and lost it.

The mistake that can sometimes be made is that we search for the same voice, when actually our experiences have altered the sound of our voice completely, so it doesn't sound like it did before the experiences that caused the loss.

I almost do not recognise the young, professional single woman I once was, living and working in London years ago, before I became a mother, before I went through a divorce, before I was married. All those experiences have changed the sound of my voice. Are there some chords that remain the same eternally? Of course.

Your voice rings truest when you have gone through the crucible because the crucible refines it.

You should always seek the sound of your voice as it should be in the present, a voice that is commensurate with your growth, your understanding, and your acceptance. You must fight the temptation to unearth the old, expired sound when a new thing has happened in your life.

To identify the sound of your voice, you listen to your heart and are not afraid to make choices different from the ones your parents or your friends have made. Your voice and path are supposed to be unique and certainly require a different and separate path to be made.

Not long ago, I became very conscious of the fact that I needed to express my voice unequivocally, but I had to find it in the new season I was in. I had to understand it and own it first before I could express it unapologetically.

My physical voice sounds different from what it sounded like in my teenage years, when I was much younger, before

I became a mother. It is the same voice, of course, but there are many layers to it; tremors and chords have shifted and refined themselves over the years. While I know it is the same voice, it isn't quite the same, and I can never get back the voice or tone I had when I was years younger.

The other day I was speaking, and I clearly heard the sound of my birth mother's voice coming through my mouth—almost like she was in the room with me, her presence so tangible I could almost hold her, even though she left this earth over ten years ago now. I paused and wondered how strange that I could hear her voice coming from me, and yet it was my voice. But isn't that the essence of those who have had the privilege of nurturing us, that their voices are so loud, they leave an indelible mark that neither time nor distance nor death could ever erase? Their goal, of course, was not to give us their voice, but to encourage us to fight for and find ours by paving the way with theirs so we aspire for better and greater.

Consider the story of Jacob as he approached his father on his deathbed to "very simply" steal the birthright of his brother Esau. For those of you who do not know this story, here is the precise version from the book of Genesis in the Bible: "But Isaac said to Jacob, Come close to me, I beg of you, that I may feel you, my son, and know whether you really are my son Esau or not. So Jacob went near to Isaac, and his father felt him and said, The voice is Jacob's voice, but the hands are the hands of Esau. He could not identify him, because his hands were hairy like his brother Esau's hands; so he blessed him" (Genesis 27:21–23 AMPC).

When I came across this passage as I wrote this book, it blew my mind because I realized yet again how powerful a voice can be—so powerful that it is recognisable by a blind father. A father who has heard me speak and knows my voice, a father who cannot be deceived by my physical appearance, but nevertheless is blinded by his love for me.

I consider how my heavenly Father's love for me has blinded Him to my sins, my wrongs, my weaknesses, but He still hears and knows my voice when I call on Him. He still longs to hear it even when it's cracked up and jacked up! Song of Solomon says: "O my dove, [while you are here] in the seclusion of the clefts in the solid rock, in the sheltered and secret place of the cliff, let me see your face, **let me hear your voice; for your voice is sweet**, and your face is lovely" (Song of Solomon 2:14 AMPC).

There is much that can happen in the seclusion of the clefts of a rock; though hidden, much can happen there. The *Merriam-Webster Dictionary* meaning of hiding place is "a place where someone or something is hidden or can be hidden." It's akin to keeping something secret. The words "hiding place" and "secret place" are often used interchangeably.

The search for your voice can be a gruelling affair, much like digging for gold, mining for diamonds, digging deep wells for water. It requires consistent effort and lots of courage; sometimes it will be painful and sometimes very uncomfortable, but oh, the sweetness of release, release that soars so effortlessly when you have found what only you possess that no one else does. Your voice.

When I began my search for my voice, I didn't even realize that was what I was doing, and so it was kind of a haphazard attempt. Hopefully, my current stage in my journey will give you a more fluent process or approach to finding yours, or at least help you polish up your search process.

Some time ago, I wrote down my personal creed and stuck it on my wall right bedside my bed. I love the words of my personal creed; they make me feel so powerful, so relevant, so invincible—and that is what the power of voice should do, not just for you, but for countless others.

Having stuck my creed on my wall, I only ever visited it on occasion, and I didn't take time to really dwell on the theme that was coming from my creed. I also kept my personal creed and the core values (family values) separate. I had created them separately and referred to them separately when actually, my values should be a product of my personal creed—if I believe that is really my life mission or purpose or dream. They should work hand-in-hand and confirm what you stand for as an individual. They should not conflict and they should not confuse but rather clarify and confirm.

There are eleven bullet points in my personal creed, and I will share the first four purely to give you an idea of what a creed would look like if you haven't a clue.

- *I am chosen, to be a life-giver, a peacemaker, a multiplier.*
- *I am a sustenance to the weary and needy.*
- *I call and I am answered. I ask and I receive.*
- *My labour is rewarded because I am diligent, disciplined, determined . . .*

I use the illustration of my creed here in voice, not in words, because a creed goes way deeper than words; it must emanate from deep within.

I am devoted to encouraging people with words of wisdom and enabling them to bring out the best in themselves as much as they allow me to. I look out for and find the best in people even at their worst. I absolutely despise unfair treatment anywhere I see or perceive it perpetuated. Where possible, I seek reconciliation rather than keeping at war by speaking the truth even when it hurts and identifying constructive solutions for all parties involved. I enjoy learning and growing personally.

All these things form part of my creed and require courage and humility, which are my core values, but I never really made this connection, not intentionally anyway. This means I never realised that in those moments when I saw something that revved my passions, identifying with my unique calling, but did nothing about it, the situation was calling on me to revert to my core value of courage and speak up even though it frightened me to do so, even though my well-being could be at risk, even when I could experience significant agony or difficulty following that moment of confrontation.

This means that at those times when a particular circumstance was so confusing and my intellect was straining to extend itself and fearful pride was threatening to shut it down, my core value of humility was urging me to simmer down. I needed to dig deep for understanding and not be in a hurry but lean into the moment. I needed to lean into the people in that situation and learn something new that would ultimately be a blessing to someone else, not just myself.

By ignoring those urges, I was refusing to dig deep and really uncover my own voice, sharpen my tone, and refine my sound day by day until it sparkled so clear and became instantly recognisable from miles away. That is the essence of our voice—that it becomes so strong, so indelible, that people who have never seen you or met you recognise your words even when they are spoken by someone else. That's powerful.

Throughout the Bible, voice is synonymous with power.

There are two dimensions to voice. The "how" and the "what"—**how** it sounds and **what** message it carries. As the owner of your voice, you need to be clear about both. If indeed voice is as powerful as the Bible says it is, we want to be very careful about the sound our voice is creating when it's released and the impressions that are being created about our self-image—effectively who we are.

I have found there may be many tones to my voice, but ultimately, its true essence will never change—my confidence in using it and lifting it to be heard is what I need to discipline myself to do correctly. Finding my voice is one of the hardest things I have had to do, but such freedom has come with it. It's the kind of freedom we were all born to experience—not buy, not borrow, just own.

Just as your physical voices change over time, so does your inner voice. As you experience different things, such as loss, love, and joy, these experiences frame your voice. The vocal fold structure is said to change with maturity, causing your voice to sound different as you age, while fundamentally the same sound is recognisable.

I think it's very important we consider the impact of our voice on our journey of self-discovery. Do you think you have a strong voice? How distinct is it? How much has your voice changed over time? Do you enjoy the vibration of your voice? How would you change it if you could?

"Loving acts as a purifier—it removes fear and every adulteration that our spirit could hold or has gathered over the cause of living."

Your Passions

Where do I begin with passions? I am, generally speaking, a considerably reserved person, but with age some of that has changed. I'm getting closer to God and knowing more of who I am and the mark I desire to leave on earth that will echo into eternity.

We hear a lot about personality types growing up. I am categorized as an introvert with a melancholia nature; an idealist with attention to detail, a love for order, and serenity to ponder and reflect, drawn to nature and beauty. What I have found is that I exist in a world that also has other personalities and dynamics, and many times I am required to operate at optimum level within conditions that my natural disposition does not equip me for. Does this mean that I eject every time I find myself in these situations? Absolutely not! If that were the case, we wouldn't need each other, but we do.

So while I have an ear to these personality tests, I am also very conscious that the voice of my Father (the spirit which is effectively the voice of God) is far more powerful than my inadequacies and shortcomings and can enable me to operate in situations my natural mind tells me I cannot operate in.

Having said that, I still have things I am fiercely passionate about, and they make me the unique individual I am. Passions are a big polisher of voice, but it takes the combination of various elements to stimulate these passions.

I thought I was living and then I gave life to a child—that has been knocking the wind out of me for years, and I am sure it will keep doing that for years to come.

When I held my baby boy in my arms when he was born, all I could say was thank you. I was thankful I had successfully carried him to term, thankful I had been able to endure the pain without passing out, thankful he was whole with no finger missing, no toe out of place. Thankful to have my body back! What was once lodged inside of me was now outside of me, but the bond was still apparent. So just as it was when it was lodged inside of me, the things affecting it outside of me still affect me even now. That bond would only get deeper having more and more access to my heart and stimulating my passions.

I grew up in a small and quiet town called Calabar in the south of Nigeria. CALABAR has been translated as an acronym that means "Come And Live And Be At Rest," simply because of the predominantly quiet and peaceful nature of its inhabitants. I attended primary school not far in driving distance from home. It was a great school with really high standards for learning at the time. I grew up in a class of boys and girls who looked just like me, and like me, they knew little of what existed beyond Calabar apart from perhaps what we saw on TV or read in books.

I was never encouraged by either of my parents to discriminate against anyone because of their social status or colour. It wasn't a thing for me personally until I grew much older and attended secondary school. My father to this day works for a living maintaining his own medical practice and trained us up on the income from that establishment. We were made to understand that we enjoyed the privilege we had because he worked hard to make it available to us. It's fascinating how we grow to miss the innocence of that age, the not knowing yet longing to know.

So when I get a call from my son's school telling me that a little boy had refused to play with him because he had brown skin, I felt as if the innocence of his age was being stripped from him. It poisoned me, but poison only served to stir up passions I didn't even know existed in me.

My son asked me once whether poison could kill you. I thought it was a ridiculous question to ask, but now when I consider it, his question was valid because not all poison is intended to kill. Sometimes poison is used to expel that which shouldn't be in you—too many doses, though, and it could become fatal. So for me, this incident poisoned me momentarily, and over time, there was a build-up as I became more and more in touch with what I had chosen to ignore over the years, which was really a systemic social construct of racism. I personally think all parties are responsible for it, and we each must strive to fight the good fight and not roll over and play dead or feign ignorance of what is happening or what has happened, for that matter.

Sometimes we stand guard over our heart and forget to feel things because we know they have the potential to hurt a lot. But what if that is exactly the feeling you need to have—to know how much you care about something and that indeed you are alive? Perhaps we need to know what it feels like to be in bondage to appreciate freedom; perhaps we need to lose a dear one to really appreciate having them; perhaps we must face financial challenges to know what it means to be without and to go beyond simply feeling and acting to initiate another's freedom. Since racism is a social construct, it is also socially deconstructed, but that deconstruction cannot happen with only one set of people. It must happen with all people, for a common good—life.

My passion is for my son to live his best life with the kind of liberty I experienced growing up as a child, but existing in what is now a global village—with no shadows or doubts hanging over his head regarding who he is or what he is capable of as a person. That passion resurrects things in me I didn't even know existed. That is what loving does to you . . . it is almost as if you exist outside of yourself with no limits to the lengths you can go.

Loving acts as a purifier—it removes fear and every adulteration that our spirit could hold or has gathered over the cause of living.

Leaning into this purification process allows us to sparkle a little more brightly.

Does it hurt? Of course, it does—every diamond could tell us a thousand tales of woe if they could speak, but all they do is sparkle because that is their voice. My passions have been uncovered and stimulated in many parts of my journey through adversity:

- Parenthood
- Personal and professional work challenges
- Financial challenges
- Losing my mother to cancer
- Losing my elder sister
- Growing up in a machismo culture
- Living in a foreign community
- Socio-economic problems that have affected the society around me

They have also been stimulated in my joys:

- Music
- Art (movies, the theatre)
- Policy, governance, structure

- Voluntary work in the community
- Raising my son
- Travel
- Experiencing new cultures

Value System

While I think psychologists are barely scratching the surface when it comes to studies on human behaviour, a few theories certainly help shed light on the deeper meaning of value systems, not just for the individual, but as we work with other people and form a part of an organisation. These are some of the aspects of being that enable us to claim our identity, as often an identity is required because it exists amongst many others.

What we do in life is work as part of a system, but we cannot work effectively as part of a wider system when our own individual systems are not clearly defined or operational. Note that I used the word "effectively" because we can work as part of a system when our value is not clear, but we would not be as effective.

Through our value systems, we put a stamp on our unique identity, and we learn to own it.

A value system is very simply a code by which a person or an organisation operates. When I think of the many interviews I have attended in the course of my career, I recall always reviewing the core value of the organisation to assess whether or not it aligned with mine. This should help a prospective employee envisage whether they will work effectively with the organisation. When we chose our individual values, we start to create our own value system.

Before you go any further into this chapter, I would like you to answer the following questions:

- What is it that stimulates my passions?
- Am I doing the things I love to do? If not, why not?
- What are the aspects of living I consider most valuable?
- What are the designs imbedded into my life that help me get through the most trying circumstances?
- What are the things I am most acknowledged for by peers, family, and friends?

If we can filter through these questions and come up with honest answers, it begins to create a pathway through and **an indication of our value system**.

There are things that remain so valuable to me—communion with God, loyal relationships, and my individuality.

There are designs that act as anchors through the most trying circumstances—prayer, discipline, and that sense of calm.

There are qualities that I am most acknowledged by my friends or peers or family—wisdom and inner strength.

A person's value system is one of the first interactions you should have with them. Very often people can get a sense of who you are by merely studying you from a distance; they may not actually have a direct conversation with you to get a sense of your values. Yet some of us don't know ourselves half as well as others do. If you are not important enough for you to take time to understand, no one will be that important either! This is a foundation building block for any value system—value yourself enough to take the time to understand yourself. People are attracted to things that understand they are valuable.

When the value system is set in place or comes into consciousness, it "attracts what needs it." The value system acts like a turbine engine would. Wikipedia describes the turbine as "a rotary mechanical device that extracts energy from a fluid flow and converts it into useful work. The work produced by a turbine can be used for generating electrical power when combined with a generator." Indeed, our value system has the ability to generate power. While we have intrinsic power, our value system enables us to generate even more that is channelled toward achieving our goals.

This attraction to our value system feeds us and continues to connect us appropriately. We are all interlinked; our journeys and experiences hold together this great big artwork that carries on through to eternity.

Even in the breaking of connection, there is opportunity for reassembly and reconnection that helps us realign. Perhaps, we have made a misstep or been driven off course for whatever reason. It still goes back to what we value most, our moral compass, if you prefer that phrase, navigating on our behalf. Consider a girl raped at the age of ten, thrown from one foster home to another because her mother could not care for her. She could choose hate or revenge as a value system, but that will not create the right connections. It wouldn't enable her to appreciate her separateness and grow through those harsh experiences. Although those things have happened, her true identity is still separate from those things.

Your value system will help paint a portrait of you to the world. Each value system is unique as each journey is unique and has something unique to reflect like the different colours of the rainbow.

The wrestles we encounter necessitate "owning our identity," which means being fully aware of who we are and owning this with its strengths, weakness, and quirks, and exploring how we can be effective in our own identity.

In this chapter, we've looked at fine-tuning or sharpening the identity we say is ours. We can see how we successfully use it to interact with the wider system around us and cultivate value in our relationships, connections, and interactions.

We also examined how we can relate in better harmony when we own our identity righteously because it attracts the right people and things to us. Owning our identity includes our voice, words, patterns, and passions. The idea is to help us in developing aspects of our lives that add value in the place we find ourselves.

We've considered how we relate at an optimum level within our environment, that is, our value system. An operative value system is used to paint a portrait of us when others interact with us, further embedding our identity in their minds.

These things will help us have a great sense of self and a restored authenticity.

Flawless Finish Pointers

- Keys for laying claim on your identity are **your words, your patterns, your voice, and your passions.**
- Your voice is powerful. Consider that out of the almost eight billion people living in the world, no one sounds the same; everyone has a distinct voice.

- Your passions are big polishers and ingredients for your voice—use them!
- Loving acts as a purifier—it removes fear and every adulteration that our spirit could hold or has gathered over the cause of living.
- Some things are best left lost!
- Grab opportunities for reinventing yourself, doing something new, stretching a muscle that has not been used. You could be pleasantly surprised by untapped potential lying dormant inside of you.
- The truer you are to yourself, the happier you will be.
- When the value system is set in place, comes into consciousness, it "attracts what needs it."

Small Group Discussion Questions

- So how do we reconcile the image or labels the world has put on us with our authentic image?
- What aspects of your life do you identify with most and why?
- What kind of risks have you taken to protect or defend your identity?
- What is your personal creed?
- Think of a situation that has presented itself to you and causes you significant anxiety or even fear. Now consider these attributes of love—patience, kindness, humility, self-control, hope, forbearance, faithfulness . . . each day apply just one element in that situation.

Chapter Four

RHYTHM
AND PACE

I've had a few art sessions with my son where we painted random projects to pass time. I've bought a variety of brushes from the shops for these activities, and it surprised me how many different types exist. Each feels different when placed on paper. Some brushes are quite thin and hard, and some are soft and fluffy, each creating a different finish and effect. These sessions have been the expeditions of an amateur, and I have been challenged to consider the knowledge the experts can offer, particularly in understanding the effects of the brush and our strokes on the canvas. The renowned Spanish painter Joaquín Sorolla is described as the Master of Light. Sorolla, according to the National Gallery, was "skilled at painting the fleeting effects of light." He was known to say, "Light is the life of everything it touches."

He also had this incredible ability to take all aspects of a singular painting and make them so congruent that it almost seemed like one object had been painted with no separation between the individual parts. Whether he was painting a landscape with people or objects in it, or painting people or objects with a natural backdrop, everything seemed to flow seamlessly as a whole.

This is the power of art, and this ability requires dynamic skill with the paintbrush. Brushes are key instruments in painting, as they help determine rhythm and pace on the canvas. Sorolla repeatedly demonstrated a mastery of the paintbrush and completely captivated the mind's eye. His play on colour to bring nature itself to life in his portraits is so refreshing. In his painting *Strolling Along the Seashore* (1909), we see the powerful impression of his brushstrokes in bringing the effect of the wind and light on the subject through the texture of paint that plays so well with colour.

Many times, we encounter elements that are beyond our ability to control. In these situations, what we need isn't brute force but a gentleness and softness that subtly changes our direction. These gentle forces are like the gentle brushstrokes of an artist.

Oscar Claude Monet is another renowned painter who used "flirtatious brushstrokes" to make his Impressionism paintings with the intent of the brushstroke capturing the light that fell on the objects, not necessarily the exactness of the objects. Monet understood that the power of his paintings was in the love he poured into them. He once said, "Everyone discusses my art and pretends to understand, as if it is necessary to understand, when it is simply necessary to love."

I consider even now the many impossible things we seek to understand when all we must do is love. In doing this, so much of the fear we often carry falls away.

When we consider paintings by Monet and Sorolla, we are schooled by their ability to uniquely utilize the brushstroke. These painters bring balance to the whole portrait by using the power of light thoughtfully, sometimes concealing and sometimes revealing, sometimes accentuating the shadows and other times catching the colours of light. There is a rhythm and fluidity to the brushstrokes by which this is successfully achieved.

Brushstrokes can be considered the intelligence of a painting. They actually give the painting its inimitable personality. This is synonymous with our individual journey laced with its milestones and checkpoints. The type of brushstroke used at different junctures on a portrait carries the ability to balance the whole picture.

Brushstrokes

When I was studying for my professional exams, I went to school in the evenings and worked during the day. I had to develop a pattern that would allow me to get the experience I needed in my field and at the same time cut out enough time in my day to learn in a classroom with other students. Even after the classes in the training college were done each term or session, I would still go to school after working hours to study before I got back home. I lived with my cousin and his family at the time, and I was considered a spirit that floated in and out of the home because I was hardly ever seen. I was up in the morning before anyone else and returned when everyone was asleep at night. Literally a ghost. Sometimes unseen, sometimes unheard, but working silently at a pace I had determined would help get me to where I desired to be.

This sometimes-unseen pace is translated in the rhythm of brushstrokes in a painting. It's not immediately obvious, but it's there enabling you to see a portrait. What might have seemed an awkward, urgent pace for some worked for me. We each need to find the pace that translates into rhythm and works for our particular situation and, ultimately, our lives. A key milestone in that season was becoming a part qualified accountant.

Have I maintained that rhythm? No, so much has changed, and so has my rhythm. What we must acknowledge is that there needs to be one to reach our milestone—we pace ourselves, and in pacing ourselves, we find our rhythm. Of course, we arrive at natural milestones in life, but even those have a natural rhythm to them which enable us to arrive at the milestone. A growing child does not just arrive at puberty; there are naturally occurring biological and chemical rhythms to the human body that get them there.

There is a rhythm to you and what you do. Find it, and in so doing, you will find others who harmonize with it.

Like the different seasons of our lives adopting different rhythms, there are different types of paintings depicting different brushstrokes.

A rhythm is defined as "a strong regular repeated pattern of movement or sound, a regularly recurring sequence of events or processes." Perhaps in adopting this, we are better able to manage and anticipate the milestones that form part of the whole plan.

Quite often, changing landscapes are presented by a milestone and understandably the rhythm you have worked with in one landscape does not necessarily work for another.

- Raising a seven-year-old son is very different from raising a three-year-old one.
- Working for an employer is very different from being an employer.
- Growing from junior management to senior management will require a different rhythm.
- Going from being a corporate professional to a media specialist will require a new rhythm.
- Being a daughter is different from being a sister.

These facets of an individual's journey oftentimes represent intrinsic parts of a whole. These facets represent opportunities to explore the full extent of their journey and their unique portrait while applying suitable rhythms that are necessary yet true to them. This is one reason why some people we may have been particularly close to in one season seem very distant in another.

What I have found really interesting with milestones is that they are very much part of a whole. Separated and standing alone, they cannot actually be described as milestone. But when this event or pillar stone is brought into the context of a whole journey or plan or strategy, then it becomes this crucial bit in the puzzle or moment in time in the story that makes a significant and relevant difference going forward and even looking back.

The Precise Landing Point

Like children, we are a generation obsessed with destination and the validity of a desire doesn't make the timing right.

When my eight-year-old son and I set off on a long journey, my son has many questions. Are we there yet? How much longer have we got to get there? He's so engrossed in getting there that many fine points of the ride are lost. We break the rhythm or pace because we are distracted and anxious to get to the destination.

There isn't anything wrong with setting our sights on a destination, but when we lose sight of the journey itself, I think we lose something significant. We might even anxiously try to speed up our journey and accidentally make another person's destination ours. In our hurry, we may miss the exits presented to our own destination, and this could be a big problem. We can sometimes get caught up in anxieties, ignoring what is present, because we long so much for the future. Alternatively, we get so caught up in the past that we neglect to stay in touch with the present.

Radiating a joyful image is inside work that starts with the present, never the past or the future. Every experience we have should be about channelling all of who we believe we are into the moment, and that habitual practice is what makes us whole. It makes us whole now, not simply for the future, but in the now.

The past and all its mistakes and faults, even its joys will always be there. We cannot change it. The present however is right before us with countless possibilities. We ought to take hold of it and squeeze. That's right, think lemonade!

When we stay focussed on being present in the moment,

every right step we take in that moment will present another right stepping stone, and that's what actually leads us to where we ought to land, not obsessing about where we need to be.

A lot of peace comes from staying in the moment; looking too far into the future can cause us more anxiety than is necessary because we cannot do and know everything about tomorrow. However, the present is here, and we can immediately identify what we can do and should do if we stay in the moment.

Sometimes I have imagined the worst-case scenario playing out because of an attitude or temperament displayed by my son. This causes anxieties and creates thought patterns that are terribly unhealthy. If we focus on the worst-case scenario for tomorrow, which has not happened, by the way, we allow our anxious thoughts to take us to places we don't want to be in or never planned to be in, and things we never intended may materialize. It all starts with a single radical thought. When our self-control does not bring a thought into submission, it can become a radical thought, rebellious and uncompromising.

Being present is not just for the good circumstances but the bad ones too. I have engaged in conversation which after introspection I knew was a real display of my lack of self-control and anxious emotions. The most powerful thing I have taken from those events has been learning the ability to isolate the issue, problem, or challenge. Once I have done that, I give myself permission to see the event with a clearer perspective that isn't muddied by past events or patterns that stimulated similar adverse emotions in me. By detaching myself from those past events and patterns, I have taken control of a large measure of my peace because my mind's perspective is focused on the present occurrence and its own variables. Isolating problematic and present circumstances keeps me from judging the situation before I have understood all of what it really is.

I still have to caution myself to be present—present with my son, present with my job today, present with my friends and family, present with myself. Our level of consciousness in the present determines our level of fulfilment in the future.

That level of presence is what defines your landing point, or the mark or the destination, if you want to call it that. That mark could very easily change depending on what you do today in the circumstances presented to you.

With regard to circumstances, there are seasons where I've had to prioritize my health, others where I've had to prioritize my friendships, and others where I've had to prioritize my job. This is also a big part of identifying with your rhythm in your season. It's okay to not prioritize social outings when that is all your best friend is doing; they're just not as well harmonized with you for that part of the journey where you need to prioritize your job or your family.

The priority is subject to change depending on the landscape or the season. This can be hard to accept sometimes when you've had such marvellous plans laid out. Yet there are some things that will always be a priority. For me, I had to realize that my health, which includes my emotional, physical, and mental well-being, is always a priority so that my son and everyone else around me can benefit from that as well.

When the painter holds the paintbrush in his hands, the

broadness of the brushstrokes change, the direction of the strokes change, and the intensity of the strokes change as well. As life is made from love, though the end is anticipated, the process is just as powerful and relevant—the patience of love is powerful, the truth of love is relevant, and the kindness of love is wonderful. When we seek to consistently apply the many attributes of love, we are being diligent, and we will be rewarded.

Our relationships and manner of interacting are such perfect indicators of where we are headed. What is even more interesting is that when we find ourselves in some of these cosy friendships that take us in certain directions, we don't always ask why we are heading in that direction, and when we end up in a place we don't want to be, we wonder how we got there. We got there by the steps we took every single day in those cosy arrangements that didn't quite challenge us in the way we ought to have been challenged.

Someone once said to me that you end up in the same place as the person you are constantly taking advice from. While I think this is largely true, I also think when we understand our separateness from others, we ask questions from that perspective to understand what we can learn for our own journey. We ask the right questions, and we seek to learn from their failures and not just their victories. Many people may counsel and focus on the things that make them look good and act like the bad stuff never happened.

One of the ways we help others refrain from making our mistakes is by telling them what we learned in the awful experience. So if you really want to learn from another person's journey, ask them what they did wrong as well as what they did right. Ask them where they failed as well as where they succeeded. Ask them what they would have done differently and ask them whether they are truly happy with their life, because at the end of the day, we all seek to have fulfilled lives radiating our happiness—not just trophies on the wall, but internal joy.

Many relationships exist in the world. We have relationships with people, things, and places, and every single thing done impacts another. Relationships help us with our boundaries, and boundaries are like checkpoints. We make boundary statements with the food we consume. For example, I don't typically drink coffee, and some people don't eat past a certain time of the night. These are boundaries put in place to support healthy relationships with food. This healthy relationship with food would in turn impact productivity levels, which translate to our pace and eventual rhythm. We make boundary statements with the places we go and the movies we watch; these habits place a check on our eye gates and ear gates. If we are not careful with our boundaries, the wrong kind of relationships or connections could be made and cultivated. When we invest in relationships with people that adversely affect us emotionally or otherwise, it most likely will negatively impact our time and the pace we are able to generate in that season. If you have a full-time job and a very busy home life as well, you need to be careful of the audience you give certain people, conversations, or situations so that a healthy pace is maintained. We may not always be successful, but I think it is important to be aware of this truth and the boundaries we have in place and make the necessary adjustments for longer-term balance and effectiveness.

Without good relationships, we exist in isolation with blind sides that we don't notice. What relationships then do is afford us the opportunity to check back on our boundaries and our personal habits and growth.

Inevitably, navigating relationships is critical in perfecting our landing point and knowing who we are. Demonstrating who we are also determines what kind of people we will attract into our lives.

Milestones

When God embarked on His creation of the world, there were milestones. The birds needed the sky, so that was created before the birds; man needed work to do, so the garden of Eden was created before he was. Each day of creation was a milestone, and there were checkpoints where God confirmed he was pleased with what He had done. We have that same ability to create an environment where our relationships as well as our milestones are optimised.

Milestones help determine the precise landing point and give opportunity for:

- Rest—After much work, you've earned a good rest.
- Recalibrating friendships and connecting—It is important to consider the connections you have made on the journey so far and whether they are still relevant to where you are going or if they are helping you become the person you desire to become.
- Reassessing plans and purpose—Plans can change, yet it is about remaining sensitive to these changes

at such important junctures as a milestone that helps with clarity.
- Rejoicing—This is about celebrating what you have been able to achieve so far.

Personally, I've had to learn a lot about celebrating my milestones. The culture of working nonstop can sometimes rob you of the necessity to celebrate your wins and your high places. While we should remain thankful at every point in our lives, these milestones call for excessive praise that are an investment into the valley moments of our journey.

What are the signs that you are getting to a milestone? Sometimes we wait for the perfect summit, the best convergence of sorts, to confirm the moment is right, but it doesn't always work that way. I have found that some of my roughest patches, the most unclear predicaments, the most unreasonable routes, were where God was moving the most and brewing the quickest. That was when the lights at my crossroads were the brightest, screaming *go, go, go*. The time was then; the wind was right. It wasn't in the structure I found Him closest; it was in the chaos, the moments of not knowing. He was there right there bleeding with me, aching with me, so that one day I would look back and say I could never have made that straight line through the maze or fog on my own.

Over the course of the last year, I have spoken to a number of truly awesome individuals, ones I honestly picked at random. These individuals are close friends and family and come from different walks of life, with very diverse outlooks on life, with their hands in different industries and so forth. Not a single one of them, in recapping their experiences or journey, plotted a clear, straight line that has been exactly as it was set out when they began their journey. Many times, they could not plot a straight line that got them where they are, but one thing was common across all of them: they believed. They believed and kept going even when the situation didn't quite make sense, because they had a conviction that what was inside of them would see them through. In narrating on the picturesque sort of life she has now, my friend said she never sat down to plot it out; she never sat to think about how she would get from point A to B. She just followed the path that kept appearing before her. Knowing her the way I do, I know she kept giving the best of herself in the situations presented to her even when she could not make sense of them, even when they broke her heart.

What do we do to prepare for the milestones in our lives? In my own journey, this is what I have discovered about milestones that also act as checkpoints about our identity. I personally think where we are is very much a function of who we are in that moment. There are six main milestones we face in our journey, whether personally or corporately. For every level or season, these milestones will present themselves over and again, taking us to the next level or season. These milestones have been further illuminated in the life of Jesus Christ in Matthew 3 and 4.

"There is a rhythm to you and what you do. Find it, and in so doing, you will find others who harmonize with it."

- **Pedestal**. The pedestal is where we know and understand by a figurehead or person of authority in our life that we are chosen for something. We have been given a designated post or territory to occupy, and we have accepted this mandate by taking position at the starting line. The next milestone cannot happen until we accept and take our position. As little children, we are put on a pedestal by our parents. It is a season where we are seen or known in ways the world will eventually come to know us and will appreciate us for, but it is a season where our parents get to nurture us. That is a pedestal season and a very important one. When we get older, we will have other pedestal moments—a new job, a new school, a new challenge, a new spouse, a new home, etc. Each of these has the objective of putting us forward to assume more responsibility, acquire new knowledge, and meet new people. (Matthew 3:13–17 AMPC)

- **Obscurity**. Moving on from the pedestal, we get to milestones where we consciously make the decision to lay low or have no choice but to stay low. In battle, this means we are kept from being seen. We do not compromise our position by drawing attention to ourselves, but we use this time to prepare for those times when we have no choice but to be seen. At this point, we are taking in a lot of information and processing it properly, so the environment in which we process when we are hidden is so critical to the success of the next few milestones. Jesus went to the wilderness so he would not be disturbed, and it was here that He experienced the temptations of His life, which set him up for the success of His ministry. When marathon runners start a race, they tend to lay low for the beginning parts of it, conserving their energy while building a rhythm that is sustainable for the long hall. (Matthew 4:1–11 AMPC)

- **Darkness**. Hopefully, we know we carry light that is meant to shine in dark places, and this is where we find ourselves in deep darkness. At this point, we are dragged down to the deepest core of ourselves to find what truly makes us so unique and cannot be changed or taken from us no matter where we go. We find ourselves among people who do not speak our language or have not experienced our culture, or we may be among people who do not understand the tools we use in being effective, such as love, kindness, gentleness, and joy. At this point in the race, the marathon runner might want to give up because their body muscles and lungs are screaming for them to stop. The purpose of being here is to test whether our rhythm is concrete enough to withstand adversity. The purpose of being here is to light up as many other lamps as we can in the process, to create a new light-filled movement and change the landscape of the portrait—change the narrative even. This is done by the way we live, not necessarily by talking or even preaching, just in the living. (Matthew 4:12–16 AMPC)

- **Teacher**. We begin to resurface at this point, having been almost buried in a dark cave where we've done much work on our core values. Now we are impacting with our actions and our words. We are dropping messages on how to do things differently. It is possible that we often find ourselves in a position where we need to impact something, but it is equally necessary that things are imparted to us where we are not teaching others but being taught. These are priceless seasons or milestones. (Matthew 4:17 AMPC)

- **Leader**. As our following grows, we need to begin to strengthen our inner circle so we can do more. Being a leader or the authority on a particular subject matter means we have experiences that people can vouch for, and they trust us because we have such a level of commitment and authenticity. Our followership does not have to exist on the Twitters or Instagrams of the world. Your followers instead could be your family, the little orphan you have decided to care for, or the elderly women you encourage every weekend. (Matthew 4:18–22 AMPC)

- **Healer**. At this point, you are living an inspirational life. Through the highs and lows, your example has touched lives deep enough to heal them and move them to accomplish things they thought they could not. They see what you've been through and start to believe they can do it too. Every act of healing starts with belief. This is the ultimate milestone; our lives are light, and light brings clarity. This clarity should grow deeper and deeper the further into the journey you go. Each time you get to this point in the journey, your circle of evolution should expand so that the next time you find yourself healing again, it is on an even deeper level. Each time you get to this point in the journey, you should be chosen for a bigger task that expands the context of your existence and all you have seen up until that moment—a shift in your perspective and what you have considered to be your horizon. Being chosen for a new task puts you on a new pedestal and gives you new sight/vision (Matthew 4:22–25 AMPC). This concept of coming full circle right back to the pedestal milestone is so profound because it confirms the nearness of God to us. As the gardener prunes the vine so that it may bear more fruit, in like manner God prunes us so new growth can occur: "Just as no branch can bear fruit of itself without abiding in (being vitally united to) the vine, neither can you bear fruit unless you abide in Me" (John 15:4 AMPC).

We prepare for our milestones by being good students, listening well, and asking the right questions. This might seem like common sense, but often we overlook the simple things.

An indication that we are definitely getting to a milestone is the landscape begins to change and becomes less interpretable because it looks new, maybe even strange.

Sometimes the language we have used in the past does not work as fluently or is less adequate because we have entered new territory; we have crossed a boundary line. Boundary lines are very interesting landmarks. At boundary lines, you we are likely to encounter natives that speak a foreign language. It's almost like getting to the boundary line of a country. Boundary lines represent crossover points and often we will see many signposts at this juncture. These signposts will tell us whether we are heading in the right direction or not. At this point, we should not simply turn around because we don't understand the language. We should read the signs. A teacher does a lot more talking than a leader does, and a healer rarely has to say anything. You cannot become a true healer without being a true leader, and you cannot become a true leader without being a true teacher. When we go from leader to healer, there is a fundamental shift in the landscape or terrain. Expectations will be different, not always right, but nevertheless, they will be there.

We might need to change our tools, in the same way the painter may need to change his paintbrushes to have a particular effect or outcome on the canvas. Or perhaps we might need to change the way we use our tools. This can pose a serious challenge where we have become comfortable. As creatures who often enjoy the familiar, this is a grave challenge for us. We need to renew the way we think about situations and stay nimble, flexible, and adaptable.

It might be a useful exercise to consider the milestones you have celebrated recently along your journey and perhaps those you haven't but would like to. More importantly, what changed in your daily patterns to make meeting those milestones possible? You should reflect on them and consider how helpful it was in ensuring that you stayed true to yourself and didn't become an alternate, unrecognisable, and unhealthy version of yourself.

What are the things you would love to change about

those rhythms you adopted? Or what are the improvements you need to make?

Do you recognise any of the milestone phases in your own life using the framework above or just generally? How has that helped you grow as a person?

I have found that depending on the area of my life, where I sit on this milestone scale depicted here will vary. For example, I could be a great teacher in my field as a finance professional, but in obscurity as a mum or vice versa. Being sensitive to your rhythm is essential to your balance.

Capability and Time

It would be remiss of me to address the concept of self-image without incorporating the concept of age. It is what drives many things in our culture and society, yet individual success or achievement are not defined or restricted to a particular age group.

We have come so far in time it is hard to believe that thousands of years ago men and women like you and me lived up to the age of nine hundred years old.

Yet in the twenty-first century, we find people strive to have accomplished all by the age of thirty and do it all over again by the age of forty! We have so accelerated our pace of life and systems for learning that the quality of time is not as appreciated as it should be or has been in times past.

I think this is one reason why the Bible urges to renew our minds, because the mind holds the ability to shed this weight we carry about whether we have done enough in the time we have. The mind has the ability to cause us to leave the necessary things behind and look to the future. It has the ability to help us heal and stay nimble and relevant to the times while exuding a whole and healthy being and this in itself helps to redefine our capability.

Our capability to move and achieve no matter the obstacles presented by age have more avenues today, particularly through channels such as social media. This social media platform is, however, the same platform that is stalking us and infiltrating the minds of our young ones with lies. It is the same channel enabling such things as "cyber bullying." This is the same channel that has led to multiple suicides, sex trafficking, assault, and outright degradation of a culture and way of living. On the flip side, this same platform has enabled people and corporations to gain back years through groundbreaking technological advancement and share those experiences so others might learn.

Through social media, we have been able to break down barriers around institutionally ingrained and adverse cultures surrounding racism, miseducation on mental health, and terrorism, for example. All these insights change our perspective on what we think is possible, even when our years don't seem to have given us the speed or trajectory we imagined.

Often, we allow things such as fashion, technology, and age to dictate the rhythm of our journey, to our detriment. These things may play a significant role in helping us find our rhythm, but they should not dictate who we are.

When I turned forty, I asked myself a very important question: What is the twenties mindset? I did this because I realized I still had so much more to give, though my vessel had become older. Though my outer man perished, the inner man was becoming stronger; my mind was becoming a lot sharper, and I wondered how I could deliver on the things I had to do with a vessel that would continue to be compromised with age. My question was fashioned to focus on my mind rather than my body, to focus on what my mind could do as opposed to what an aging body could do.

When I was growing up, my parents tended to celebrate some key birthdays. These included your tenth birthday because you had you first decade behind you, your eighteenth birthday because you had pretty much become an adult in your own right (usually we had our first glass of wine at this age), and your twenty-first birthday (not sure why this one was special, but it was). And from then on, it was the multiples of ten that were most relevant because you had put yet another decade behind you.

So getting to forty was definitely a milestone moment where I guess I subconsciously wanted to keep up the tradition of celebrating a new decade. Also, the next decade would bring me to the halfway mark of fifty. At this point, I was thinking, *How do I operate at a higher level of performance and build on what I know now while carrying the dreams I carried when age was saying, "You might want to slow down"*? My twenties represented an age of exploration and opportunity to discover a lot of things around me as well as within me, but as I grow older, I realize that never stops. It is sometimes that our sense of curiosity is doused by experience, yet curiosity is important to having the right capacity for advancing.

Often how we personally feel about our age is down to what we think we are capable of. Our capability is very simply "the power or ability we have to do something." It indicates who and what we can influence, who and what we can develop, and who and what we enable or bring some kind of change or empowerment to. As humans, we gain so much confidence in this knowledge because it means we need not rely on someone else to do it for us, and that is powerful information to have and cultivate.

The twenties mindset presents a sense of invincibility. It is an age where most people come into full independence and at the same time acquire a reasonable degree of information for living. There is almost a sense that life will just go on forever—the end isn't in sight, so the mindset of enjoying the moment with very little care of tomorrow is so much more potent. As we get older, whether as a sense of responsibility or experience, we tend to be more cautious about the way we live life.

When we are younger, we are learning so much about the world and we are so open to new experiences. But as we age, we begin to form set patterns that tend to reduce the elasticity of our brains. This means we suffocate curiosity. To really dive into who we are, we must stay curious by asking ourselves the simplest questions and not making assumptions about who we are, because who we are is an ongoing revelation.

- Why did I respond that way to his comment?
- Why was I upset by my daughter's questions?
- Why did I use those specific words to describe the situation?
- Why do I have a fear of swimming?
- Why do I dislike the taste of raw fish?

- Why do I find it easier to listen than to speak?

Sometimes we use age to define or set our milestones of achievement, and while that may be helpful, it doesn't always work out that way.

On January 30, 2022, the reigning Miss USA Cheslie Kryst apparently jumped to her death from the twenty-ninth floor of her Midtown apartment building in New York. At thirty years old, she was a lawyer, a pageant queen, a TV host, and part of a big family. One would never think "high-functioning depression" when describing her. So why do I bring this up?

Our ability to function as a whole being has very little to do with our physical appearance or how long we have walked this earth; rather, it is a function of the level to which we have accepted ourselves and learned to love ourselves. People who suffer from depression believe they are deficient in some way.

The very sad end of this Miss USA is a reminder of how important mental health and well-being are, especially given the stupendous rate at which we have trained ourselves to function in society today. The COVID-19 pandemic has revealed some of those frantic and unnecessary patterns. It has revealed this too: We were not built to function at the alarming rate at which we are operating. If it took God twenty-five years to work his purpose through Abraham, who was one hundred years old, why should we try to cram all our achievements into thirty years or forty years? It took David twenty-two years from the moment he was anointed to the moment he became King of Israel.

One of the comments associated with Kryst's reign as

Miss USA was that she was too old to hold the title. This is a typical example of how we use age to define our success and levels of achievement. This is what we often use to drive ourselves, forgetting there is a journey to be experienced.

On average, the human now lives as long as sixty-six years. In the days of Abraham, humans lived as long as nine hundred years. This is fact, according to the Bible. There are many reasons why we could not possibly live up to that age now—the way of life is completely different. Our diet, for example, consists of significant amounts of processed foods, while people of long ago ate mostly natural and fresh foods directly from the farm, with no preservatives or fertilizers. The people of long ago had very simplistic goals, including marriage, raising a family, and focusing on their craft. There was less pollution, if at all, from the environment that we breathe on a regular basis. Our ancestors were not stalked by cyber bullies or oppressed by what they saw on social media. They were busy building their immediate communities, which were tangible sources for belonging and community. Today, however, we find ourselves dealing with significant carbon emissions that pollute the air we breathe. The hype of this technological age was absent thousands of years ago and was therefore not a hazard to human health or longevity.

The present day poses many threats to our physical and mental health, which accelerate our age. Sometimes this acceleration is not commensurate with the level of confidence or assurance we need to have about ourselves.

Society will have its expectations of us, but I believe the deepest and truest expectations you set are those you have arrived at by getting to the core of who you are truthfully and being 100 percent okay with what you find there.

In this chapter, we have explored the brushstrokes of a paintbrush as they practically apply to the rhythm and pace of our own lives. Rhythm and pace, I believe, are critical aspects of art. The idea is to create a lifestyle balance that suits our unique identity by understanding its importance.

We mustn't get so caught up with the destination but learn to appreciate the milestones in between, and this sets us up better to pace ourselves and embrace the journey. There are six milestones highlighted in this chapter using the context of the life of Jesus Christ in Matthew 3 and 4: Pedestal, Obscurity, Darkness, Teacher, Leader, and Healer.

I believe Christ's desire is that our lifestyle flows seamlessly as a whole, while remaining congruent with our heart, our unique value or abilities, and of course, the final destination.

A big part of developing our own rhythm and pace is in considering our relationships and being present and sensitive to changing landscapes or seasons as these will accentuate our unique self-image.

Flawless Finish Pointers

- There is a rhythm to you and what you do. Find it, and in so doing, you will find others who harmonize with it.
- Our relationships are such perfect indicators of where we are headed, but the execution (understanding and application) of our

singleness, our separateness, keeps us on our unique course.

- Radiating a joyful image is inside work that starts with the present, never the past.
- One indication that you are definitely getting to a milestone is the **landscape begins to change.**
- There are six main milestones to moving forward in our journey: Pedestal, Obscurity, Darkness, Teacher, Leader, and Healer.
- Often how we personally feel about our age is down to what we think we are capable of.

Small Group Discussion Questions

- Was there ever a phase in your life when you knew you had to change the way you communicated in order to get ahead? What was that like? How did that challenge your growth?
- Name some of your favourite people and why they are your favourite.
- What active steps do you take to being present? How often do you practicalize these steps?
- Do you make a habit of celebrating your milestones? Why?
- Which milestone stage do you think you grow most in? Which do you appreciate the most?
- Do you have any expectations for yourself? How did you arrive at them?

Chapter Five

THE POWER OF REFLECTION

The Italian brothers Annibale and Agostino Carracci were some of the first artists in the 1590s to draw exaggerated portrait sketches, which were caricatures, for fun. "The word "caricature" comes from the Italian words *carico* and *caricare*, meaning "to load" or to "exaggerate." Caricature is the art of capturing a likeness of someone, through a method other than pure representational portrait, and usually with an aspect of humour. The artist's goal is to emphasize specific features that make a person unique.

Caricatures have been used for centuries, in newspapers, magazines, and blogs as part of political movement, and have triggered controversy and illuminated personality in art, history, literature, and many other facets of society.

Publications such as *Vanity Fair, The New York Times, Time* magazine, and *The Economist,* to mention a few, constantly use the caricature to translate their views more swiftly to the reader.

In my season of writing this book, I've realized how predisposed we are to do or believe just what others have said about us. How others see us and the plans they might have for us can be like a caricature. Another person might focus on a certain aspect of us, not our whole self. If we allow another person's view of us determine how we define ourselves, then we are possibly not operating out of our authentic self. I had initially wanted to call this chapter "Societal Expectations," because the art of intimacy is effectively about getting to know ourselves deeply and truly, and sometimes part of that journey is getting over the expectations set by others around us—our family, our society, our friends. We have to shed all consciousness that attaches us to false loyalties because in being untrue to ourselves, we do ourselves and others a disservice.

Still, the art of intimacy will require time for reflection, which is powerful in and of itself. Emphasis should be placed on not forgetting what we have found. Choosing to forget what we have learned about ourselves is almost like choosing to be lost. As long as we remember, we can never be lost because we recall truth and knowledge, and ultimately, we recall power.

There are many ways we can see our physical reflection—mirrors, water, glass. Each of these present an object through which we see ourselves and through which we observe other objects around us. Depending on the type of material, we could be presented as still, flowing, or blurry. We could be reflected as we are or in almost a caricature-like version of ourselves. I mention this to say that not every reflection of ourselves we encounter is altogether true or precise, but ultimately, it shows us a likeness of ourselves. Yet it isn't simply a likeness we are seeking. It would be absurd for one to say they didn't know what they looked like, for only the blind can afford this luxury.

To encounter a reflection true or false, there must be an object to reflect it. This is the same with us. We have objects in our lives that present and suggest to us what we look like, and ultimately, what we are. Taking time to understand the objects we have chosen for this exercise is important because if the object is subject to inaccuracies, in turn, our reflection will also be inaccurate. The cerebral reflection of our core, our ideologies and beliefs that define who we are, is what I refer to here.

I enjoy art in its many forms—paintings, drama, music—and every one of these forms of art have evolved in so many ways. Paintings are quickly becoming one of my favourites. A painting reveals so much in a split second. What it reveals could be different depending on who is looking at it, along with their perspective and even their mood. You don't have to be an artist to slap colour on a piece of paper and call it art, but you will need to be a seasoned artist and creator to get a portrait right. The human portrait is a classic form of painting, and this has evolved over time.

The question that follows from that is how do we know when we are distorting our self-image? How do we know when we are not being real, authentic, and who we are meant to be along the path of becoming?

We can start by looking to the right counsel. I have been and continue to be such a sensitive person, yet I know how important it is to receive counsel, and sometimes that counsel will provide you with a snippet of what you look like that you may not have thought to consider. I also get the opportunity to counsel others and I observe how blinded we as humans can sometimes be. If you choose to go down this route, certainly do not do this in isolation, even when the source is tested and true. Even they are susceptible to contamination resulting from something or someone in their lives. The source for reflection needs to be tested and true for the right counsel to flow from it. Test the waters or wells they drink from, because the level of contamination in the water will likely show up in their assessment of people and things around them.

It is wise to have a few views on something rather than just one, because combined you have various wise perspectives that point you in the right direction. The Bible confirms, "Where there is no (wise, intelligent) guidance, the people fall (and go off course like a ship without a helm), But in the abundance of (wise and godly) counsellors there is victory" (Proverbs 11:14 AMP).

Caricature

When I was eighteen, I went to university in Nigeria. My university was almost six hundred kilometres away from home, which is equivalent to just over five hours travelling by road. I had never attended a school that far from home.

University was like its own republic, with its own government and set of rules by which the students lived. Like many young men and women, I was very much loved by my family, yet one becomes like a prey in the wild when you enter into institutions such as these, a statistic existing in a different terrain from any one might have known before. I suppose for the current generation coming up, "GEN Z," this sort of experience might start as early as high school.

When you leave the comfort and safety of home to go to college or university, you almost are transported into a different universe where you become another registration number in a huge pool of multiple backgrounds, personalities, agendas, and cultures. No one really knows who you are, and you have left behind the ones who managed to own a part of you because so far you have grown up around them. Here you are, simply another individual with the same corporate goal as every other individual passing through that educational system. In fact, you could say you have become a target, depending on what others see in you.

When I attended university, you left the home nest and experienced this very different terrain with its diversity of people from multiple backgrounds and associations. The current generation, however, doesn't need to leave home to experience this. They may have this experience sitting down on the sofa at home. This republic of becoming a random statistic has chased them down into their own homes and foundational educational institutions and is already presenting an alternate understanding of their self-image, already attempting to groom a false self-image before they have left the nest.

The extent of this experience does vary from generation to generation and from geographical location to geographical location. I had quite a sheltered upbringing, so university represented an opportunity for a kind of liberation, and therein existed the crisis of twisting one's identity or self-image if one was not careful.

I suggest a kind of liberation because liberty as a concept is often misunderstood. It is often assumed liberty means we can do what we want to do, but actually, true liberty or freedom is doing what we "ought" to do. When we refuse to do what we ought to do, over time, we end up in bondage, and our overall sense of well-being could be severely compromised.

Like many people while in university, alongside academic learning, I experienced heartbreak, wrong choices, and of course, prejudice, but far above all those things is something else I got, which I will never forget and still have—the opportunity for true friendship. Friendships are vehicles that determine much about the journey we experience and the direction we are going in.

Some of the best friends I have come from my time in university, which is ironic because I had some painful experiences in university too, and even though I do not live in close proximity to these friends now, our hearts are bound by the friendship forged in those sometimes tremulous years of our journey.

Understand this: heartbreak is a crack in our subconscious. It is a disappointment that arises because we have put our trust in someone or something that did not understand or appreciate our value/worth. Many times, we go through life without allowing that crack to restore itself by forgiving ourselves and, of course, forgiving those we think have hurt us. We must acknowledge the truth that we are still loved. When we carry this crack around for extended periods, it results in more cracks that widen and could cause severe damage to us. We are driven to introduce addictions that are temporary and superficial, only solving the surface problem rather than the root. These unseen crevices forming in our hearts and minds have the ability to twist our true reflection of ourselves. They have the power to twist our true self-image and inhibit our expression. This is the hidden pandemic we face in the world today; it is the pandemic that is flooding the system. No one is really talking about this because it is so pervasive. The twisted self-image is basically a caricature.

After so much time, fine lines and cracks have formed on the *Mona Lisa*, and artificial substances have been required to stall the natural decline of the painting. Our true self-image is not synthetic in nature, and our decline is not stalled by the introduction of artificial substances or preservatives. It is stalled or reversed by the Word of God. The Word is light that shows the way, its water that refreshes, its oil that nourishes. This is how we identify with our authenticity.

The effect of the caricature prevents us from identifying with our true self-image—it is a cracked-up and jacked-up image, contorted and distorted. Essentially, it's a lie and sometimes even comical. This image is often weighed down or deflated.

Our true image is balanced, nimble, and blazes a trail with fire, burning up the distortions and contortions that our world may want to dent us with.

True Freedom

Misuse of our freedom leads to a twisted self-image. When we misuse our freedom, we have most likely:

1. Been stifled with rules and legalism. This is really dangerous ground to be on. Legalism drives us to despondence, but grace elevates us. Freedom requires that we know what we ought to do, and we do it. When we are made to feel despondence or strive to reach an unattainable bar with little or no grace, we will flounder.

2. Been stifled with the need for perfectionism. No one is perfect. Often in our attempt to be perfect we put others down and we are overly critical. We are easily provoked and find it hard to see the good even when it's in front of us. We have little or no gratitude for what we do have. Discovering our true self-image is about appreciating what we have while we reach for better with grace.

3. Misappropriated our resources, including our time. This also means we end up misusing our relationships, misusing our talent, and misusing our money. Inevitably, we end up misusing our health and minds just to gain balance back.

The misuse of freedom results in a struggle to gain back the balance we believe we have lost in some way. Sometimes, if we are not careful, we end up a lot further out of balance. Consider the scale of some of the wars fought over the centuries, all in an attempt to win back some kind of freedom, yet resulting in major drawbacks in economic, social, and financial liberties.

My first major crack happened because I gave my time to a relationship that fed me lies, and perhaps in naïveté, I imagined that would free me from legalism. More importantly is the fact that my conviction about who I was could not sufficiently hold me up firmly in those interactions. The conviction that I was already free was not fully manifest. I didn't have the conviction that I did not need some sort of romantic attachment to give me that freedom. I already had it. I was already free to live my best life and make righteous choices that were mine.

How we spend our time is an indication of how much we value and understand freedom. In this day, we spend a lot of time trying to find things that satisfy our vanity and give us social status. While there is nothing wrong with social status, we compromise much in regard to our authenticity in trying to be fit for our society. We should be fit for our purpose, not the purpose society dictates to us, and these two things might be very different. True freedom understands this.

True freedom understands grace, not legalism; true freedom knows what ought to be done, not what people or the norm expect should be done. True freedom does not only appreciate and savour the now but also eternity. The ability to differentiate comes through grace, and even this will vary in measure in one's life, even though it has been made abundantly available to all.

We live in an age of the twisted self-image; it is prevalent and pervasive. It is actually the number one pandemic that is not actively being treated, yet it requires the most attention because it is responsible for so many premature deaths to our dreams, so many hate crimes on our uniqueness, suicides to our growth, and abortions to our seed. By turning a blind eye on this distortion of our self-image, we are enabling a suicide of our original mission. We become an accomplice to the abortion of our God-given vision. These are statistics we will never know because many may never realise they were living a lie.

Statistics report that over 6,000 people in the UK committed suicide in 2020, and in the US, approximately 46,000 committed suicides and another 1.2 million attempted to take their own life. Many of these have resulted because of a dream buried or forgotten, a crime on their uniqueness— be it race or culture or sex—a stifling of their growth, or the death of a seed placed in their hand. Many of these are preventable if many were given the opportunity to truly cultivate and reflect their authentic self.

We can't translate this to mean that we will have no difficulty or challenges in being true to ourselves, because we will. But hopefully, those discomforts will be filled more with grace and peace. The discomfort we feel in distorting our self-image leaves an unnatural heaviness, an ache for more because of the hollowness of the life we might be creating. We feel the hollowness because we don't know how to fill up a vessel that is contradicting its purpose or imitating the purpose of another. We can only be the best at who we really are. A vessel that has been twisted cannot be filled to its original capacity. Our true source is unable to fill a vessel that is contradicting its original mandate.

The world needs our authenticity, not a caricature of who we are. Caricatures may create a lot of comical relief but very little substance, very little generational fruit, very little healing, if at all. The world needs what we were originally designed to carry. The world needs all the different colours, voices, passions, and creativity that we have to bring, and we should bring it with gumption to relieve us from a grievous end.

The best thing we can do is consider our own heartfelt desires and bring them under the light that never fades away, the light that is constant and chases every shadow. The light that illuminates our path to glory. We need to be honest with ourselves, be brave, be determined, and not give up on ourselves, knowing we are more than enough!

We need to identify with people who are chasing their authenticity, find people who are not afraid to not conform to the norm, find people who love truth, find people who will be honest with us and not just play the cheerleader for cheering sake. We must choose wisdom and understanding and apply it to our lives.

"Choosing to forget what we have learned about ourselves is like choosing to be lost. As long as we remember, we can never be lost because we recall truth, knowledge, and ultimately, we recall power."

Lessons in powerful reflection

Powerful reflection requires bravery and a conviction to rewrite the dominant narrative. The power of reflection lies in the truth of discovering our unique flair that ignites and harmonizes beautifully with others.

Graciousness is a product of sincere and powerful reflection because we do not only come to understand our fragility but the fragility of others as well. When you are able to see a piece of yourself in everyone you meet, your humanity is awakened; without this, it is impossible to sincerely relate.

My journey of intimacy continues every day. It doesn't stop as long as I keep permitting the entrance of truth, as long as I keep open to the learning process.

A while ago I decided to embark on a new experience: skiing. I would absolutely love to go skiing in Switzerland. The thing is, I knew absolutely nothing about the sport apart from the fact you get to go really fast through a blanket of snow. I imagined the feeling of exhilaration as I did that, and so skiing went on my bucket list, and it had to be Switzerland because it had to be in the Alps. Plus, I had always wanted to live in Switzerland.

I showed up late for my seven-hour lesson with about seven other attendants, and for the first half of the lesson, I was about the only one who fell over repeatedly with no clue how to stabilize myself in the awkward ski boats we were all wearing. By the last fall, which seemed pretty awful, I was asked to stand on the side to catch my breath while my instructor continued with the rest of the class. I felt terribly humiliated, and if I hadn't acknowledged it before now, I was conscious of the fact that I was the only black woman in the class. In fact, when I looked across the skiing rink at the other classes taking place and the people attending, I could not see anyone who looked remotely like me. While this hadn't mattered before, it mattered now, because already I was feeling separate from the class because of my repeated falls, which were no fault of mine, of course, but I began wondering whether there had been some secret memo given out before I got to the class or something the others knew that I didn't. I remember asking a few of the attendants whether they had skied before, because they seemed to balance so effortlessly.

On reflection of that day, it became apparent to me that when we find something that sets us apart from others, we naturally begin to look for the next thing and then the next thing, and it goes on and on until we are forced to isolate ourselves because we think no one would understand us or really see us. The truth is that this happens the other way round as well, where we find a commonality between us and the next person and then we find another and then another, and suddenly we realise we are not that different after all, even though on the surface it might seem like we are different. It was so easy for me to forget the cheerful smile of one of my classmates who cheered me on and asked me to join again after I had been benched because I had fallen so hard on my side. It was easy to forget the number of people who extended help when I couldn't get up because of the weight and angle of the ski boots. It was easy to forget the lady I bumped into who said, "It's okay, we are all learning," after I apologised so profusely. All I could see was how different I was on the surface because that was most attenable as a reason, yet many of the things that bind us as humans are not immediately attenable. So that requires a bit more digging, searching deeply to find truth about ourselves and each other.

The other reflection on that day was more about balance and how we are sometimes unaware of the balance or imbalance we create in our lives. Skiing is one of those sports that really does expose how well your physical frame is balanced, whether you are left-legged or right-legged. First time I ever heard such terms in my life. I know about being left-handed, but left-legged? No. Until then I had never considered that I walked mainly with the right side of my body, so I am heavily inclined to my right leg. The implication of this in skiing was that I found it hard to lean to my left ski boot so I could "turn to the right" on the slopes. I was still struggling with this when the class ended.

This was frustrating, but have you ever considered that perhaps there are some areas in our lives where we might be out of balance or leaning on other aspects too heavily, which make it hard for us to take the necessary turns in another direction as the landscape changes along our journey? Has it ever occurred to you that maybe the challenge is simply you are slightly out of balance and need to take some time to deeply reflect on what you are really working with?

Another really powerful reflection from that day's lesson was the fact that I had gone into this class without bothering to find out about the outfit/regalia! This was all provided, of course, but I had little understanding of the peculiarity or necessity of what I would be wearing for the lesson. The ski boots, I found out eventually, are quite a unique set of shoes like none I have ever come across both in design and weight. They are as heavy as they are ugly! Still, the knowledge of those boots determines much of the experience you have on the slopes. I learned that the boots include a huge Velcro strap that lays across the shin and buckles that hold them in place when the boots are put on. Velcro is actually a trademark and the material itself, according to the *Collins Discovery Encyclopedia*, is "a fastening consisting of two strips of nylon fabric, one having tiny hooked threads and the other a coarse surface, that form a strong bond when pressed together." This strap acts like a brace round the front of your shin all the way down to your ankle, and this keeps you from falling forward. It also helps to keep you firmly attached to the boots, so when you fall it can be a huge struggle to get yourself up on the slopes. I could lean forward as far as I wanted into those boots and I would never fall or lose balance, but the minute I leaned back or sideways, I began to lose control. This was a huge learning point for me because it created awareness of the level of control I had when I had initially felt like I had none. In fact, when I leaned into my boots on the slopes, it propelled me forward; the more I leaned in, the faster I went.

This is like the Word of God to me. When I lean in, I am propelled forward; when I lean away, I tend to feel stuck or get stuck and make the clumsiest mistakes, stumble, and sometimes fall. It is in leaning in that I have protection and indeed adequate control of the situation because I know I am in my faithful Father's hands. I use the word "adequate control" because just like skiing out in the snow, I know I can control which way I go, but I cannot always anticipate what the weather or terrain would be like out there—that is out of my control.

In discovering who we are, there is much we can take

responsibility for when we reflect deeply, and in doing so, we create the right equilibrium, not just for our journey but in those of many others.

The product of true reflection is not necessarily what others have to say about us but what we have to say about ourselves when we do this in close relationship with God. How to reflect powerfully is certainly an art, and I have shared my own experience of how I have done this within a simple but deeply challenging and new experience. I have shared my outlook on the situation, my preparedness, and my response all happening in my mind and driving my outward projections on this life experience.

The age-old art form of the caricature is an interesting one that helps to illustrate the challenges we might face in seeing our true self-image and shows us how sometimes a twisted self-image is presented. At the heart of a healthy self-image is a spirit that is truly free.

A big part of disarming the false self-image is understanding true freedom, being set free from false loyalties, and allowing our hurts to heal properly.

In this chapter, we also explored the concept of a hidden pandemic resulting from cracks that have been left uncared for (not watered) or insufficiently oiled through the journey. These cracks can be especially dangerous and detrimental to the fruit-bearing image God desires for each and every one of us. These cracks or experiences could hinder us from identifying our true image. Instead of being caught up within the dangerous cracks of what this pandemic might present, let us reflect powerfully:

- Remember your mind has already been saved from every kind of darkness this world could present. When you understand that your mind is saved and has the capacity to hold content that stirs the cause of your life, you have a new appreciation of your self-image.

- Remember you are able to do the right things not because of your own acts but because of what the One without blemish has done.

- Remember when you talk, walk, and work, believing for things you cannot yet see, you are defying the odds present circumstances may suggest to you. Faith has the power to cast aside and burn up distortions and lies concerning who and whose you are, and it opens deep reservoirs that help build up your true image.

- Remember to wear peace in everything you do, to seek peace, to strive for it. Peacemakers are born of righteous acts, and righteous acts are not always quiet acts, but they will seek the good of all concerned to cultivate harmony and unity even where differences abound.

- Remember to seek the truth and speak the truth. Truth holds it all together. If you lie, the seams begin to fall away and you are exposed. Exposing yourself to consider a lie is one of the most dangerous things you can do to your self-image.

There are people we have been called to, people our light is made to reflect on, and the only way to reach them is by first being well yourself. We do this by consistently pursuing a clear understanding of our mission, our self-image, our value.

A caricature does not stand a chance in this war for lives. It will not provide effective administration of the required medication, nor will it trigger the generational blessings that need to be triggered because the effects of their design are only fleeting, momentary, and consequently ineffective.

Alternatively, our true self-image will wage war and win many victories. It will provide effective administration of the required medication. It will trigger generational blessings because the effects of its design are eternal and effective.

Flawless Finish Pointers

- We have to shed all consciousness that attaches us to false loyalties because in being untrue to ourselves we do ourselves and others a disservice.
- Choosing to forget what we have learned about ourselves is like choosing to be lost. As long as we remember, we can never be lost because we recall truth, knowledge, and ultimately, we recall power.
- We can only be the best at who we really are. A vessel that has been twisted cannot be filled to its original capacity.
- The misuse of freedom results in a struggle to gain back balance we believe we have lost in some way. Sometimes, if we are not careful, we end up a lot further out of balance.

Small Group Discussion Questions

- What is the worst possible impression you've had of yourself and why?
- What is the best possible impression you've had of yourself and why? How often do you act on this impression?
- How do you practice forgiving yourself and others?
- How often do you intentionally purge your mind of negative things people might have said about you or how they see you?
- What does authenticity mean to you and how do you practice it?
- What does truth mean to you and how do you practice it?
- What does freedom mean to you and how do you practice it?
- What liberties do you think you have lost and how have you tried to gain them back?

Epilogue

We may all seem ordinary at first glance, but perhaps if we took the time to be a little more intimate with ourselves, we'd feel more appreciation for our uniqueness.

When I looked at the *Mona Lisa* that day, at first glance, she seemed ordinary, but then I stood for a little while. I allowed her gaze to meet mine so that we were the only two people in the room. I caught her essence; her eyes carried this acknowledgement of her deep sense of worth, not in a prideful way but almost bashful and bold at the same time. It was a look that promised she would never be deterred from that knowledge.

I often think of *Mona Lisa* as the woman in Proverbs 31, a woman of noble character. Even though mystery surrounded her, just as mystery surrounds each of us, she was a faithful wife—a woman who brought no harm to her husband but rather glory. Even through a painting, hundreds of years later, she communicated the beauty and essence of who she was, and it has been imprinted on those who have seen the painting.

I believe each of us is a creature of immeasurable

value. The revelation of our true identity keeps unfolding. We are trustworthy and we are strong. We are incredibly industrious as well as kind. We are exceedingly creative and full of wisdom.

Our choices matter, so we need to be mindful of them. Our dreams matter, so we must fulfill them. Our heart matters, so we must guard them fiercely. We aren't simply more than enough. We are flawless.

About the Author

Ekanem is a woman with great depth, a lover of Christ, and an advocate for wholeness and empowerment who is passionate about writing and enjoys travelling and meeting new people and experiencing new places. She remains enthusiastic about discovering herself and taking other engaging minds along on the journey. She enjoys trying new cooking and baking recipes. She is also a qualified accountant with the Association of Certified Chartered Accountants.

Ekanem is a mum of an energetic eight-year-old boy and they live in Wakefield, West Yorkshire of the United Kingdom Being a mum is one of the greatest achievements of her life and continues to surprise and grow her every day. It has opened up many avenues for friendship and networking as well, one of which is the Amazing Mums (AM) network, a group of mums building community online and in person to support each other on the journey of motherhood and womanhood.

Ekanem's love for writing began when she was in primary school and although she didn't nurture it much then, she kept a diary for most of her teenage years and in her twenties, she found her way back to journaling by starting a blog called the <u>elegance of souls</u>.

Her love for writing is the basis of her podcast, *theeleganceofsouls*, and her guest list remains quite niche and close to home. Every conversation on the elegance of souls is inspired by her writing, reflections on lived experiences, her quiet time with God, art, nature, and the diverse cultures, people, or challenges we might encounter each day. As a podcaster, Ekanem seeks to give encouragement, insight, and empowerment from her own challenges and through community and faith.

Printed in the United States
by Baker & Taylor Publisher Services